Mind skills for managers

Mind Skills

FOR
Managers

Samuel A. Malone

Gower

Mind Maps® is a registered trade mark of the Buzan Organization Ltd.

Published by
Gower Publishing Limited
Gower House
Croft Road
Aldershot
Hampshire GU11 3HR
England

Gower
Old Post Road
Brookfield
Vermont 05036
USA

Samuel A. Malone has asserted his right under the Copyright, Designs and Patents Act 1988 to be identified as the author of this work.

British Library Cataloguing in Publication Data
Malone, S. A.
   Mind skills for managers
   1. Self-help techniques 2. Self-management (Psychology)
   3. Personal information management 4. Life skills
   I. Title
   658.4'093

ISBN 0 566 07817 1

Library of Congress Cataloging-in-Publication Data
Malone, Samuel A.
   Mind skills for managers/Samuel A. Malone.
      p. cm.
   ISBN 0–566–07817–1 (cloth)
      1. Executive ability. 2. Management—Psychological aspects.
   3. Communication in management. 4. Interpersonal communication.
   I. Title.
   HD38.2.M355   1996
   858.4'09—dc20   96–15513
                                                                           CIP

Typeset in Great Britain by Bournemouth Colour Press Ltd., Parkstone, Dorset and printed in Great Britain at the University Press, Cambridge.

Contents

Preface

This book is about the critical skills that you need in order to prosper in your management role or in your personal life. It is aimed at people in all walks of life who want to give themselves the competitive edge. It emphasizes the mind skills that are necessary for successful living. The book is not designed to be read in one go, but rather to be dipped into as the need arises.

The book has twelve chapters, each of which is self-contained. There is a Mind Map® summary for each chapter which should be previewed before reading the chapter.

Chapter 1 deals with how the human brain works and is a brief overview of that most complex and mysterious of living organs. Chapter 2 is about basic adult learning skills which will help you become a better and more effective learner. Chapter 3 tells you how to apply problem-solving skills in a business and personal capacity. Chapter 4 is about creativity and how you can become more creative. Creativity is a skill which is needed in many areas of business life. Chapter 5 tells you how to use memory more effectively to improve recall. Chapter 6 is about Mind Maps® – a revolutionary note-taking technique invented by the psychologist Tony Buzan and now used by many in business and education.

Chapter 7 is about effective reading and how you can train yourself to become a faster reader while improving your retention and comprehension. Chapter 8 is about effective writing: a critical skill for managers. Chapter 9 is about how to manage your time, a skill necessary in your business and private lives. Chapter 10 is about public speaking which is important if you want to get to the top in business. Many people rank public speaking as the greatest fear in their lives, so becoming proficient in this area is a worthwhile accomplishment. Chapter 11 is about the art of human relations. Being able to get along with people is critical in business and everyday communications and will help you live a happy life. Interpersonal skills are now thought to be more important than technical skills if you want to progress in your career. Finally, Chapter 12 tells you how to manage stress. Maintaining the proper balance between work and leisure is necessary for mental health and a long and prosperous life.

The skills in this book must be practised. The best approach is to take one idea at a time and apply it. Then take another idea and put that into practice and so on. By this method you can become proficient in a wide range of skills over a planned period of time. Knowledge will never become your own unless you use it. Practice makes perfect and practice makes permanent. Good luck in your efforts to acquire 'Mind Skills for Managers'.

Samuel A. Malone

1 How the brain works

- What is the capacity of the brain?
- How do the hemispheres of the brain specialize?
- What are the effects of relaxation and diet on brain function?
- Does the brain deteriorate with age?
- What are the techniques to integrate left/right-brain processes?
- How can we learn from the great brains of the past?

Brain capacity

Psychologists now estimate that most people use less than 1 per cent of the brain's potential. The brain's potential is determined by the number of connections it can make with 10–15 billion nerve cells, each one capable of making thousands of contacts. The possible permutations of connections run into trillions. Previously it was thought that we had about 10 billion neurons, but more recent research estimates the number of neurons at about 30 billion and the area of the brain at about 2,200 square centimetres. This gives us some idea of the vast capacity of the brain and its potential for learning if properly used. The average brain weighs about 3lbs, about 2 per cent of body weight, but takes 25 per cent of the calories we consume. It produces its own painkillers and even generates about 12 watts of electrical power.

Three parts

The human brain is divided into three basic parts: the reptilian, mammalian (or limbic system) and the cortex. Although the parts have different functions they do interact and affect each other. These parts developed during different periods of our evolutionary history and together are called the triune brain. As you may have guessed, we share the reptilian brain with the reptiles. This part of the brain is in charge of the five senses. The fight or flight and survival instinct with its concerns for food, self-preservation, shelter, reproduction and territorial instinct are located here.

We share the mammalian brain with all mammals. The mammalian brain surrounds the reptilian brain and contains your feelings, pleasure sensations, memory and learning ability. Your biorhythms, such as sleep, hunger, thirst, blood pressure, heart rate, sex drive, body temperature and chemistry, metabolism, and immune system are also dealt with here.

Higher intellectual skills

The cortex is the part of the brain which gives us our unique human characteristics. It wraps around the top and sides of the limbic system and accounts for about 80 per cent of brain matter. The cortex is divided into two hemispheres, each covered by a one-eighth of an inch thick intricately folded layer of nerve cells. The hemispheres are connected by a large structure of 300 million neurons called the corpus callosum. Because of the cortex, we are able to plan, organize, remember, communicate, understand, appreciate, and create. These are the higher intellectual skills and differentiate man from the other primates.

Brain hemispheres

Early left/right brain research was mainly conducted by Roger Sperry and his associates on split-brain humans. Briefly, split-brain humans have their corpus callosums surgically cut to control severe epilepsy. It is through these experiments that psychologists began to understand how the brain's hemispheres work. In 1981 Roger Sperry received the Nobel Prize in Physiology/Medicine for this research. Since then there has been much speculation about the implications of this research for education, training and development, learning, memory and creativity. Long before this it had been established that the speech centres, called Broca's area and Wernicke's area, are located in the left brain, which controls the right side of the body.

Specialization

Based on this and other research, many psychologists believe that the brain's hemispheres specialize in different areas. The left is the logic side, dealing with language, problem solving, convergent thinking, computer programming and so on. The right is the artistic side, dealing with creativity, imagination, divergent thinking, face recognition and so on. Although writing is considered a left-brain skill, it is now known to require the cooperation of both hemispheres. The verbal aspect of writing is logical, but the actual process of writing uses motor and visual skills. Learning to use computers is a left-brain skill as it tends to be sequential, orderly and logical. Computer programming obviously fits into this category, although systems analysis would combine both logical and creative skills and require an integration of both sides of the brain. The ability to form an overview, or the 'helicopter view', a skill needed in strategic planning, would be a right-side capacity.

The integrated brain

The two halves of the brain may be specialized, but they are not isolated – each complements, interacts with and improves the performance of the other. Although the brain is bifunctional, the most productive and creative intellectual functioning occurs when both are talking to each other. This integration can be helped through appropriate learning experiences that encourage the simultaneous processing of information from both hemispheres. The left hemisphere controls the right side of the body. Research shows that damage to the left, or dominant hemisphere results in poor performance on tests for verbal ability. It also controls language and logical activities which operate sequentially.

The right hemisphere controls the left side of the body. Damage to the right hemisphere results in people doing poorly on non-verbal tests involving the manipulation of geometric figures, puzzles, completion of missing parts of patterns and figures, and other tasks involving form, distance and space. It directs spatial, simultaneous things and artistic activities. Research has found that the left dominant hemisphere is anatomically larger than the right hemisphere and is more active than the right in most adults.

The brain expands with use

The brain is the only organ that expands through use. The more it is used, the more memory associations are formed. The more associations are formed, the easier it is to remember previously acquired information, and also to form new associations. Research shows that although no new nerve cells develop in the brain after birth, new synapses do seem to grow and develop. The connections between neurons form the brain's circuits and networks. The major circuitry of the brain is laid down by birth, but the details and fine tuning continue to develop throughout life. Indeed, experience itself can cause new synapses to grow. Experience, then, can shape the brain.

Some psychologists think that information in the brain is processed in parallel rather than serially, in line with modern computers, artificial intelligence and expert systems which now mostly use parallel processing. This theory suggests that learning can be improved when the input of information takes this form and supports the use of diagrams to present information in chunks facilitating integration and overview.

Learning how to learn

In western society, because of the emphasis on the traditional educational system, our logical brain tends to be highly developed and dominant. However, our creative brain is comparatively neglected. Obviously it is a great advantage to know your brain, how it works and how to use it effectively. Many new educational programmes around the world now focus on how to improve the mind's operation through 'learning how to learn' skills. In a rapidly changing world, with new techniques coming on stream frequently, it will be more important for people to know how to learn. Most people now change careers several times in a lifetime, making it essential to learn new skills quickly. Peter Drucker, the management writer and consultant, says that the business executive of the future must be someone who knows how to 'learn how to learn'. In science and technology a graduate's knowledge is out of date within a few years. Hence the need to know your brain and how it works in order to go on learning.

Although we now know a lot more about the brain than at any time in history, we still know very little. The brain is the most complex and mysterious living organ on earth. The important thing is to be able to use the knowledge we have about the brain to help us become more effective lifelong learners.

The brain and age

Scientists in the past thought that the brain only grew until we were in our late teens. However, it has now been found that the brain does not reach its maximum weight until we are about 30 years of age. Better news still is that the integration of the right side with the left side is not fully developed until we are 40 years of age. Although there is some evidence to suggest that the brain does deteriorate after 60, this deterioration is very gradual. So there is no excuse for anyone not actively learning until ripe old age. Poor attitudes rather than deterioration in brain power is the main reason why many people give up formal learning when they get older. The more you learn the more developed your brain becomes. The more developed your brain becomes the greater capacity for more learning.

Use it or lose it

Roger Sperry's work demonstrated that when people develop a particular mental skill, it improves all areas of mental activity, including those that are lying idle. In other words, you can be both creative and logical and using both sides of the brain improves overall intellectual performance. Learning and experience can cause new synapses to grow in the brain. The brain is therefore like a muscle – using it makes it grow and develop and keeps it in good shape. It seems to be a case of use it or lose it.

Relaxation and diet

The way in which the brain specializes has been shown by measuring its electrical activity. When relaxed the brain tends to show an alpha wave rhythm, when active a beta wave rhythm. Ornstein found that a subject doing mathematics showed an increase in alpha in the right hemisphere. Thus the right hemisphere was relaxing and in an alpha wave pattern, whilst the left was active and in a beta wave pattern. In contrast, when a subject was matching coloured patterns, the left showed alpha (i.e. resting) and the right showed beta (i.e. active).

Relax and learn

Relaxation is now accepted as an important element in accelerated learning. Numerous studies have found that anxiety can be successfully reduced through relaxation training and that learning and creativity is helped. Dr Georgi Lozanov uses relaxation and music to induce a state of mental repose so that material is more easily absorbed, learned and retained. Many scientists have come to the conclusion that the key to more effective learning may lie in the limbic system. The limbic system, as previously explained, is that part of the brain which controls the emotions, and an appeal to the emotions is the most effective way to create attention and memory.

Scientists have found that relaxed individuals have a feeling of drowsiness which is usually accompanied by dreamlike images and reverie. This period occurs between sleeping and waking and happens only 5 per cent of the time for most individuals. It is during this drowsy state between sleeping and waking that people have unique insights, and that very creative people are able to bring about this reverie or insight state at will. For example, Thomas Edison had some of his greatest insights on waking from 'catnaps'.

Brain food

The brain needs nutrition to function. Protein, carbohydrates, lecithin, and vitamin B1, in particular, are needed for good brain functioning, so make sure you take a good varied diet if you want your memory to be at its best. For example, nutritionists have found that both intellectual and emotional functioning is enhanced by eating choline, which is found in fish, liver, soybeans and egg yolks. This seems to support the old story that eating fish is good for your brain. Choline is a component of lecithin. High dosages of lecithin improve the recall ability of individuals with poor memories. A study by the US National Institute of Mental Health revealed significant memory increase in normal adults taking 10 grams of choline daily.

Vitamin B6, which is thought to improve the transmission rate of neural signals within the brain, has been found to be effective in improving memory. Ginseng is thought to improve learning, memory and concentration. Researchers have also found that drinking lemonade containing glucose right after studying facilitates later recall. Apparently, glucose helps with the chemical processes that register long-term memories in the brain. The possibility of brain food and pills to enhance learning and memory function is no longer a dream and a breakthrough is likely within the next few years.

The brain needs affection

In addition to proper nutrition your brain also requires love and affection, oxygen and information. You can provide love and affection by frequently feeding the subconscious positive thinking and visualization. The brain takes 40–50 per cent of the oxygen supply, so make sure your work environment is adequately ventilated. Without information to stimulate the brain, it will atrophy and die. People have been known to become senile through lack of mental stimulation.

Great brains of history

The great brains of history were people who were able to combine both sides of their brain. It is very noticeable that the great scientists combined imagination and intuition with logic and analysis. It was the partnership of right and left brain that made the crucial difference. Einstein visualized what it would be like to travel on a sunbeam. He then transformed his dream by logic into provable formulae. We would not be enjoying the benefits of many electrical gadgets without the persistence and creativity of Edison. Kekule, a German chemist, discovered the molecular structure of benzene while dozing in front of the fire allowing the pattern of flames to inspire him. Da Vinci displayed both scientific and artistic talents and anticipated many modern scientific advances. To be successful in life, visualize your goals and follow your dreams just like the great brains of history.

Techniques to integrate left/right-brain processes

Most people have a preference for one thinking style, i.e. left-brained or right-brained. Accountants, engineers and lawyers tend to be left-brained, whereas artists, entrepreneurs and strategic planners tend to be right-brained. Depending on your learning style preference you should try and develop the brain skills that you underutilize. For example, left-brained individuals could use the following techniques to integrate both their left and right brain skills and thus optimize the effectiveness of their brain.

Music and rhythm

Music and rhythm are right-brain functions. Classical music and baroque music in particular has been found to facilitate learning. Jingles, rhythms and rhymes, as advertising practitioners are well aware, facilitate the learning and retention of advertising messages. The same concept can be used in training and development. Baroque music played softly in the background could be used to create a relaxed atmosphere.

Visualization

Visualization is a right-brain function. Psychologists have found that individuals who visualize a finished product or end result are most successful in achieving their goals or solving problems. In a training and development situation, learners should therefore be encouraged to visualize the end product or result as vividly as possible.

Diagrams

A picture speaks more than a thousand words. Learners should be encouraged to represent ideas and concepts in a diagrammatic form. Diagrams simplify problems, facilitate overview and encourage right-brain processing.

Emotionalize

The more emotions are involved, the more the information will be registered in the right brain. Information which is processed by both the right and left sides of the brain is more likely to be remembered. Experiential learning employing as many senses as possible facilitates right-brain processing.

Make analogies

The right brain likes metaphors and analogies. Using comparisons from different disciplines will stimulate right-brain processing.

Mind maps®

Mind Maps® use both sides of the brain. The words and logic of Mind Maps® call on left-brain skills. Their radiant, non-linear format, with diagrams, pictures, symbols and colour, call on right-brain skills. So by drawing Mind Maps® you integrate both sides of your brain.

Humour

Humour draws on left-brain, rational processes and on right-brain creative processes. The inclusion of humorous material in learning situations will help to integrate both sides of the brain. When you laugh your brain secretes endorphin, a natural hormone which has a painkilling and tranquillizing effect on the body. The result is a feeling of well-being.

Other techniques such as relaxation, biofeedback and creativity also enhance right-brained thinking.

Summary

- The capacity of the brain is enormous. Psychologists maintain that we use only about 1 per cent of the brain's capacity.

- The brain is divided into three parts: the reptilian, mammalian and cortex. The reptilian brain handles our sensory motor functions, survival and fight or flight instinct. Our mammalian (or limbic) system handles feelings, memory, biorhythms and the immune system.

- The cortex handles our higher thinking and is divided into two hemispheres. The left brain is the logical side, while the right brain is the artistic side.

- Relaxation has a positive effect on the brain and facilitates learning and creativity.

- The great brains of the past displayed both logical and creative abilities.

- Techniques which encourage right-brain activity include music and rhythm, visualization, diagrams, use of emotions and making analogies.

- A good diet is necessary for proper brain functioning. Certain nutrients and vitamins have been found to improve memory.

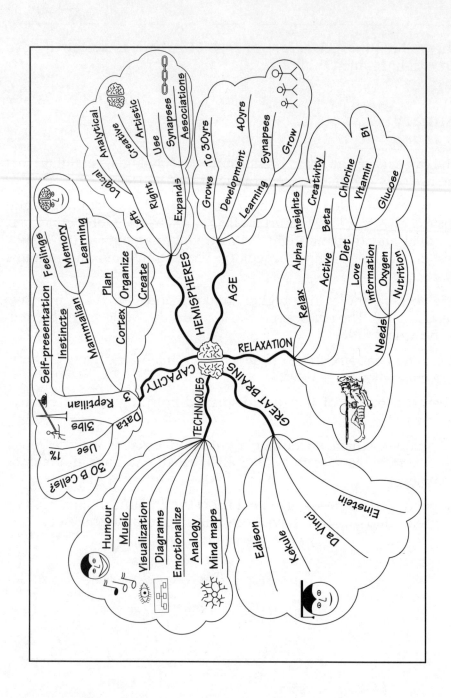

Chapter 1 How the brain works

2 Adult learning skills

- Why are objectives and feedback so important in learning?
- How can I create a supportive environment?
- What are the six Cs of successful learning?
- How does age affect learning?
- What are the basic laws of learning?
- Why are learning styles important?

Introduction

There are now more adults engaged in training and development and part-time educational programmes than ever before. Most of them have full-time jobs so it is important that they know how to get the most from their time and that they know some of the skills of learning. If you buy a computer you are given a very detailed operating manual on how to use it. Your brain, the most complex living organ on earth, comes with no operating instructions. Because of change people now need the skills to learn quickly and effectively.

Unfortunately our educational system teaches us how to be taught rather than how to learn. We are passive rather than self-directing learners.

Motivation and feedback

Learning means change. It has been defined as a change in behaviour resulting from experience. Learners are able to do something that they were unable to do before. To learn you must be dissatisfied with your current state of knowledge and skill and be prepared to move forward to some desired new state of competence. To move forward you need motivation backed up by energy, enthusiasm and persistence. There are two kinds of motivation – intrinsic and extrinsic.

Intrinsic motivation

Intrinsic motivation comes from within. It may be fuelled by interest, challenge, the need for self-esteem or the need to become self-actualized. The following phrase sums up the idea very succinctly: WIIFM – What's In It For Me? In other words, how useful, beneficial and meaningful will the learning experience be to me?

Extrinsic motivation

Extrinsic motivation may be fuelled by the need for social approval, the desire for higher remuneration or promotion or the need to keep up with one's peers. Intrinsic motivation works better than extrinsic motivation, but both combined would be a strong inspirational force. Obviously if you're doing something because you are inherently interested in the topic, it is a very strong motivational force. On the other hand, dislike for a subject has a negative motivational effect on learning. Expectancy theory suggests that adult learners will work hard if they believe that they will be rewarded and that the probability of success is high. Whatever the source of your motivation, the diligent plodder often succeeds where the lazy, but brilliant person fails. Thus low levels of motivation can result in poor academic or on-the-job performance, even in very able people.

Feedback

Feedback or knowledge of results is gaining information on how well you are doing on the learning task. It assumes you can measure your progress against performance standards at appropriate stages of learning. It is thus linked to goals and sub-goals. Sub-goals are milestones on the way to the main goals and are essential because the more immediate the feedback the more motivational it is. Feedback acts as reinforcement of successful learning and positive reinforcement works better than negative reinforcement. Success breeds success and success is, of course, its own reinforcer.

Feedback is a type of check or control on your performance and a way of putting things right. If you are doing well you can build on your success. On the other hand, if you are not doing so well you can analyse the reasons for your substandard performance and take corrective action to put you back on the right path again. Feedback at the end of the learning process is too late to be constructive. Feedback needs to be frequent, early and timely so that the corrective learning strategies can be put in place quickly. Small successes help you stay motivated.

The learning environment

Accelerated learning is based on the concept of making the learning environment as supportive as possible. It emphasizes the use of classical music, relaxation, visuals, positive feelings and the subconscious. The idea is to stimulate and involve as many of the senses as possible, including sight, hearing and touch. The learning environment can be enriched with plants, art, colour and music. Baroque music, played softly in the background, has been found to create the right ambience for relaxed successful learning. The colour scheme should reflect a warm and friendly atmosphere. Seats should be arranged in a circular or horseshoe shape to facilitate interaction and communication between participants. The whole emphasis is on making the learning environment as informal as possible. Accelerated learning is in fact a more holistic approach, by borrowing and combining ideas from the various theories of learning.

Attitude and learning

Adult learners often have negative attitudes about formal learning situations inherited from unhappy experiences during their time in school. To counteract this the psychological learning environment should be supportive and non-threatening. Learning should be fun, never boring, threatening or judgmental. Learners should be reassured that the learning will be easy, relaxing and enjoyable. Some stress is inevitable and can in fact sharpen the mind and focus concentration. However, high levels of stress can block learning, hence the need for a non-threatening environment.

The Escort model

The ideal psychological climate for learning should have the following characteristics. Use the mnemonic ESCORT to help you remember them.

Enquiry   Learners should be encouraged to ask questions and take responsibility for their own learning by becoming actively involved rather than listening passively.

Support   The trainer or facilitator should create a climate of support and encourage interaction and assistance from peers. Learners sometimes come to training situations with negative attitudes and anxieties about losing face in front of colleagues.

Collaboration   Adult learners have great experience which they should be encouraged to share with other participants. The emphasis should be on teamworking rather than competition.

Openness   Learners should be encouraged to be open, frank, natural and honest. In other words they should be themselves.

Respect Adult learners crave recognition and respect. They don't like to be talked down to or treated like schoolchildren. They want their experience to be recognized and acknowledged.

Trust Trainers should view their role as facilitators in the learning process rather than as authority figures. They are there to help create a climate conducive to learning and build up mutual trust and rapport with the learners.

The six Cs of successful learning

The six Cs of successful learning are Curiosity, Confidence, Commitment, Concentration, Conviction and Celebration.

Curiosity

Children have an inherent curiosity about everything and an amazing capacity to learn. They have the habit of prefacing everything they say with the marvellous word 'why?' They want to know the reason for everything. This process can be embarrassing to adults who sometimes cannot answer the questions posed and so often respond in a negative fashion. As a result the child eventually gives up asking these questions and so the natural curiosity is stifled rather than encouraged. To become successful learners we must rediscover and re-ignite this natural curiosity for knowledge and learning. Some of the most amazing discoveries in history were prefaced by the word 'why?' Seeking out answers to questions is an active form of learning rather than a passive form and is thus more effective and meaningful.

Confidence

Confidence is the belief that you have the innate ability to learn in formal and informal situations. On the other hand, lack of confidence is synonymous with self-doubt, negative attitudes and self-imposed psychological limitations. Self-confidence is the first requisite to great undertakings. Build on your strengths and work to eliminate your weaknesses. Think about the successes you've had in life rather than dwell on the failures. See new learning situations as a challenge and potential opportunity rather than a threat.

Commitment

According to Disraeli 'the secret of success is constancy to purpose'. Persistence is the trait which often sees people through in the end. Commitment must be real and be supported by time, energy and enthusiasm. For example, it would be impossible to complete a professional accountancy qualification successfully without investing the huge time and energy commitment to study and work. It's a combination of ability and hard work which gets you there in the end.

There's a phenomenon in learning theory called the learning plateau. In a new learning situation there is initially a rapid rate of progress, followed by a slower rate of progress. This is followed by a stage of no progress where stumbling blocks appear which seem to be insurmountable. Some learners give up when they meet difficulties, not realizing that these same problems are experienced by all learners. This is useful to know because it will save you feeling inadequate and frustrated and make you realize that you are no different from anybody else. Positive thinking and encouragement at this point in the learning process can mean the difference between success and failure. The art is to persist and see a way through or indeed around the obstacle. After that there is then fast progress to a higher level of expertise.

Concentration

Concentration is learning how to cope with, manage and eliminate distractions. Use creative visualization to get rid of irrelevant thoughts, concerns, daydreams and negative feelings. Visualize yourself learning successfully. Psyche yourself up to the learning task by saying to yourself 'My concentration is very sharp'. 'I am fully concentrated'. 'Every day in every way my concentration gets better and better'. Nothing will focus your concentration better than the actual process of beginning the learning task.

Conviction

Conviction is the belief that you can do it. Concentrate on the end result (where you would like to be) rather than on the process and difficulties of achieving it. It is the prospect of achieving a clearly defined goal which will mobilize your enthusiasm and commitment. See yourself as being successful with the benefits that will ensue as a result of your success. The 'Pygmalion effect' or self-fulfilling prophecy suggests that you achieve what you expect to achieve and that adult learners tend to live up to their own and others' expectations.

Celebration

Occasionally you need to pat yourself on the back. Celebrate your little successes and completions. This will create positive feelings and give you the encouragement to go forward relaxed and determined and building on your success to date.

Age and learning

The good news is that you can learn at any age. In healthy adults up to the age of 70 there is very little fall-off in the capacity to learn if you go at your own pace and in your own way. It is the speed of learning rather than the capacity to learn which declines. Studies show that older workers are just as productive as their younger colleagues and indeed often have a better work attendance record. However, as one grows older reaction speed slows down, you tire more easily and your eyesight and hearing are not as sharp as they used to be. In practice, most people adapt and compensate for these changes.

Biological life-cycle

The biological life-cycle traces the stages people go through during their lifespan: birth, growth, maturity and decline. There is no doubt that the physical senses do decline as one gets older, but fortunately in healthy adults the rate of mental decline is very gradual and is hardly noticeable until ripe old age. There are plenty of examples, reported in the news media, of senior citizens graduating from university, which proves that it is never too late to learn and that you can teach old dogs new tricks.

There is little fall-off in creativity with age, as exemplified by Picasso and G.B. Shaw, both of whom produced good work into their nineties. B.F. Skinner, the learning theorist, produced outstanding work into ripe old age. Similarly, in the professions there is plenty of evidence that older more experienced practitioners are better at solving complex and subtle problems than their younger less experienced colleagues.

The ability to learn is often an attitude of mind. If you feel insecure and threatened by new learning situations it is unlikely that you will be a successful learner. If you treat new learning opportunities as a challenge rather than a threat you are more likely to be successful. Keeping mentally and physically fit will maintain your capacity to learn. Keep your mind active by setting yourself new learning challenges from time to time. The brain needs oxygen to keep in shape, so a vigorous walk now and then will keep your mind and body in shape.

Overall intelligence improves with age

Educational psychologists divide intelligence into fluid and crystallized. Fluid intelligence is your ability to perceive complex relationships, form concepts and use your short-term memory. Crystallized intelligence is acquired intelligence, through education, upbringing and knowledge. Some fluid intelligence abilities such as short-term memory decline with age, but the rate of decline is minimal and is more than compensated for by the increase in crystallized intelligence. For example, the slight decay in short-term memory can be aided by the use of mnemonics and other memory techniques. Similarly, wisdom, which is an example of crystallized intelligence, improves with the years. Hence judges and chief executives tend to be middle-aged and older.

Basic laws of learning

The mnemonic DEEP AIR will help you remember the seven basic laws of learning: Disuse, Effect, Exercise, Primacy, Association, Intensity and Readiness.

Law of disuse

If you don't practise a skill or recall and rehearse knowledge it will eventually be forgotten. Forgetting has nothing to do with age. It's just a consequence of not reviewing. The forgetting curve is a well established and proven theory in learning. The period immediately following the learning process is the most important time for reinforcing knowledge. A review schedule should be drawn up, with reviews about ten minutes after the learning event, after 24 hours, after 1 week, after 1 month, after 3 months and occasionally thereafter to revise and prevent the natural process of decay. Learners should also be encouraged to reflect in order to consolidate and integrate new learning with their existing knowledge and experience. Mind Maps® which concentrate on essentials should form part of your review plan. Remembering can be enhanced threefold by the use of visuals. The old 'show and tell' concept is still very effective.

Law of effect

You are more likely to learn and pursue your learning on a longer-term basis if you find the learning process pleasant, satisfying, enjoyable and rewarding. In formal situations, people often give up learning because of unpleasant associations with previous occasions, like being made to feel inadequate by trainers or educators. With adults the trainer's role should be more facilitating rather than directive; they should provide all the encouragement, reassurance and support that adult learners often badly need. Make sure the learning environment facilitates learning. Remember the term 'information overload'. If you try to cover too much in one session your audience will become confused and unable to cope. Concentrate on the essentials, rather than clouding the issue with too much detail. Take frequent breaks for rest and reflection. Be aware of the idea of biorhythms. People are usually more alert in the morning, while in the afternoon they tend to be more sluggish before they pick up again. Presentations are thus better given in the morning, and the more participative approach such as role play and case studies are better in the afternoon.

Law of exercise

The more often that you do something, the more proficient you will become in doing it. Practice makes perfect – if the practice is the right kind. Doing something the wrong way can become a habit which you may find hard to break, so make sure you are doing it the right way. In school you learned your arithmetic tables through repetition or overlearning until they went in to your long-term memory. Now your recall of these is automatic. Similarly, the operations involved in driving a car, after a period of time, become an automatic response which you do without thinking leaving your mind free to attend to other matters as you drive along.

Law of primacy

New things or things that you do first are remembered better. This is the novelty concept at work. Likewise you remember that which is unique and outstanding. Also actions that you do last are more lasting. In-between things are more inclined to be forgotten. The more participation and involvement you create for your learners the more likely they are to learn and remember. When learning a new subject you can capitalize on this principle by consciously increasing your powers of observation and concentration during the early stages of the process and actively engaging all your senses including writing and doing during the process.

Law of association

Adult learners learn by linking and associating new knowledge to prior knowledge and existing experience. Association is therefore the basis for most of our learning. Techniques like Mind Maps®, previewing and the SQ3R method act as advance organizers by facilitating the acquisition of new concepts, knowledge and information.

Law of intensity

If the learning experience is dramatic, exciting and memorable it is more likely to be remembered than if it is routine and boring. Consider for a moment what you remember about your holidays? Very little, except the unique, outstanding and funny incidents. Good trainers have a reputation for bringing their subject alive. They do this by relating their enthusiasm to the learners' experience and by the use of discussion, example, anecdote, analogy, metaphor, story, illustrations and good visuals. The greater and more intense the interest of your learners, the more effective the learning process will be.

Law of readiness

You can take the horse to the water, but you can't force it to drink. Adults must be able, willing and ready to learn. Unless the adult is innately motivated and ready to learn, the best efforts of a trainer will be to no avail. Trainers should always emphasize the importance of the topic, how it relates to the experience and goals of the learner and how it can be used to improve job performance. Case studies, simulations, demonstrations, role play, management games, practical exercises and group discussion will all make the learning experience more realistic and relevant to adult learners. They will also help the transfer of learning to on-the-job situations. Frequent summarization during the learning session will help retention and recall. The more variety of approaches to learning, the better.

See the big picture

Trainers may facilitate adult learning by progressing from the general to the specific and from the simple to the complex. Give the big picture first and then fill in the detail. The learning material should be broken down into manageable units. Adults with frequent, longer and more recent educational experience will tend to adjust better to a learning situation than those without such benefit. Remember adult learners have a fund of experience and by sharing it with others a synergy effect will happen. They can learn as much from each other as from the trainer. Indeed, the trainer can also learn a lot from them. For adult learners learning is a means to an end rather than an end in itself.

Adults learn from many different resources including books, magazines, newspapers, cassettes, videos, television, films, computer-based training, experts, role models and peers. They tend to persist and learn better if they like and are comfortable with the preferred resource.

Learning styles

People have different approaches to learning. Some are interested in theories and concepts, while others prefer the practical application of ideas. Adult learners in general like to involve themselves actively in the training process, like to share their ideas and experiences and tend to be self-directing and problem-centred. Some learners are more left-brain dominant, while others are more right-brain dominant. This means that some are analytical and rational and prefer logical and sequential learning experiences. Other people are creative and artistic and like plenty of interaction, visual experiences and role play. A good trainer will try and cater for this by using a variety of techniques which appeal to both the rational and artistic parts of the brain and to as many of the senses as possible.

Summary

- The role of objectives, feedback and a supportive environment are very important in facilitating effective learning.
- The six Cs of effective learners are:
  - curiosity
  - confidence
  - commitment
  - concentration
  - conviction and
  - celebration.
- The basic laws of learning which can be recalled by the mnemonic DEEP AIR are:
  - Disuse
  - Effect
  - Exercise
  - Primacy

- Association
- Intensity and
- Readiness.

- The trainer must produce a psychological climate conducive to learning.

- The characteristics of such an environment can be recalled by the mnemonic ESCORT:
  - Enquiry
  - Support
  - Collaboration
  - Openness
  - Respect and
  - Trust.

- Trainers should have regard to the learning styles of learners if they wish to be successful. Adults generally need more flexible, participative, experienced-based and problem-centred training.

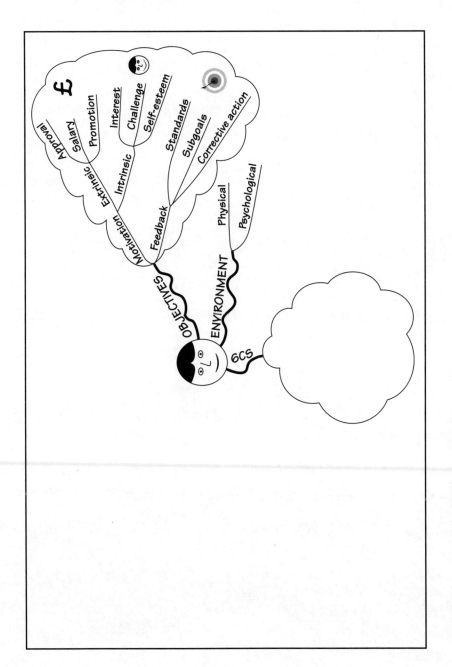

Chapter 2 Complete this Mind Map®

3 Problem solving

- What is the SREDIM approach to problem solving?
- What factors should I consider when choosing alternatives?
- What should I take into account when collecting information?
- What is the systematic approach to analysing data?

SREDIM

In organization and methods, which is work study applied to the office, there is a well-known approach to problem solving which can be recalled by the mnemonic SREDIM:

Select the problem for study. Identify the problem. Make sure that you understand what the real problem is.

Record the facts. Differentiate between facts, assumptions and opinions.

Examine, analyse and interpret. Adopt a critical, questioning and sceptical attitude as appropriate.

Develop alternative solutions. Flexibility of mind and creativity is needed here. In how many different ways could this problem be solved?

Implement. Put into operation the best alternative or combination of alternatives.

Monitor and follow up to ensure that your solution has worked out satisfactorily.

Select and identify the problem

Identify the problem, or problems and issues involved. Identify the real problem. Einstein wrote: 'The formulation of a problem is far more essential that its solution, which may be merely a matter of mathematical or experimental skill. To raise new questions, new possibilities, to regard old problems from a new angle, requires creative imagination'. Do not confuse the symptoms with the problem. For example, an influenza virus causes a headache, sore throat, sneezing, tiredness, perspiration and aching joints. These are symptoms – the action of a virus which is the problem. However, identifying the symptoms may help you to identify and solve the problem.

Gap analysis

What is a problem? In very simple terms it is the difference between an actual situation and some desired state. Problem identification is therefore the gap between the present and the desired state. The gap is filled by implementing appropriate strategies.   Another way of looking at a problem is to say that it is some undesirable situation that needs to be resolved.

The first step in the identification process is to understand the existing situation. The second step is to compare this with the desired state of the organization. Remember, there is likely to be more than one problem facing the organization.

The position audit under the eight Ms classification may help you to identify the main problem categories. The eight Ms are Manpower, Money, Materials, Machines, Management, Management structure and culture, Marketing and Management Information Systems. State the problems as precisely as possible. Crystallize the problem in writing. All problems will not be of equal importance. Prioritize your list of problems by focusing on the solution of those with the greatest payoff.

Question the problem

Problems are usually interlinked and interact and affect each other in a complex multifaceted manner. Ask yourself – What is the problem (or problems)? Where does it occur? When does it occur? Whose problem is it? Why does the problem occur? What are the reasons for the problem? How can the problem be overcome? Organizational problems may be caused at corporate, functional or line level: by poor performance or standards in planning, leadership, motivation, control, communication, coordination, objective setting, time management, delegation, interpersonal relationships, interdepartmental conflicts, organizational politics, discipline and many more. Remember, a problem well stated is halfway to being solved.

Record

Focus on the facts appropriate to the solution of the questions raised. Ask yourself – What facts do I have? What facts do I not have? What additional facts do I need to solve the problem? How much will it cost to learn these facts? How urgent is the decision? Can I afford to wait for these facts? In practice, most decisions are made with incomplete information. Recording and gathering facts is a very time-consuming and expensive business. You must clarify in your own mind the objectives and purpose of the exercise. Ask yourself – Why am I collecting these facts? You must be able to differentiate relevant from irrelevant data, which calls for considerable judgement and experience. You must also devise the best and most economical way of collecting the facts.

The systems approach

The systems approach is a useful mental philosophy and framework to help develop an organized method of collecting facts in administrative problems. A business is an open system and is, of course, part of several bigger systems. It exists in a dynamic environment and must continually learn and adapt to its environment. No business is an island unto itself. A system has inputs, throughputs and output, with repeated cycles. In a manufacturing business the inputs are human resources, raw materials and machines. The throughput is the manufacturing process and the output is the finished product. Similarly, an office may be considered as a system with its own inputs, throughputs and outputs. The ratio of input to output is in fact the productivity ratio. The office itself is but a subsystem of the firm. The systems within the office are but subsystems of larger systems. They all interlink and impinge on other systems.

When considering a problem against an office background you must realize that the office is a complex system – not only an administration with its own inputs, throughputs and outputs, but also with other systems (human relations etc.) impinging. One can quantify the inputs, study the throughput processes and methods and see what the final product or service is. Systems should of course be studied from start to finish and followed through all their stages. If a system is changed, repercussions on other systems should be considered. This is what is meant by a total systems viewpoint.

Interviewing

Interviewing and observing staff is a good way of finding out what is going on in the office. In recording information from interviews remember that things are not always what they are said or appear to be. There are in fact four different viewpoints and interpretations of the 'actual situation'. Verify the actual situation by direct observation and flowcharting. The system is not necessarily what the office manager says it is. The office manager may be twice removed from the actual work done and therefore is not talking from direct hands-on work experience. The clerk doing the work will in all probability tell you not what he actually does but what he thinks you want to hear. Procedure manuals and standing instructions are what is supposed to happen, but of course these can also be wide of the mark.

You must maintain the highest standards of impartiality, integrity and objectivity when interviewing staff. You must not be seen to be taking sides. You must maintain a mid-course with objectivity at all times. Develop good listening skills and be aware of the barriers to effective listening. Briefly these barriers include prejudgement, jumping to conclusions, assuming that other people think as you do, lack of attention, having a closed mind, wishful hearing, semantics, excessive talking and lack of humility.

Tips for interviewing

Try and break down barriers of suspicion and resentment. To win the willing cooperation of staff you must actively involve them on your side. Here are a few interviewing tips which may help you to win over acceptance:

- Never argue. Avoid emotive issues. Remember you may win the argument but you may lose the cooperation of the employee – 'A man convinced against his will is of the same opinion still'. Be diplomatic, even if the employee is thoughtless, difficult, abrupt or rude. It is not your job to reform the employee. Your mission is to establish the facts.

- Show respect for the employee's opinions, no matter how obtuse they seem from your point of view. Never tell an employee directly that they are wrong. There are more diplomatic ways of winning them over to your viewpoint without making them feel small.

- If you are wrong, admit it before the employee takes the opportunity to tell you.

- Always be friendly, sympathetic and appreciative when dealing with staff. Give credit when due.

- Start the interview on the issues on which there are mutual agreement, thus laying the foundation for further trust.

- Let the employee do most of the talking. They know their job better than you do and may have plenty of ideas just waiting to be released.

- Use the employee's ideas and let them know that they are their ideas. Even if they are not the employee's ideas, make them feel they are. This will generate cooperation and smooth the way for implementation.

- See things from the employee's point of view. If you were standing in their shoes what would you think? Empathize.

- Be sympathetic to the employee's ideas and wishes. If you meet them halfway, the greater the chances of getting the changes accepted and implemented.

- Dramatize your ideas. Visuals can be used very effectively in an oral presentation.

Plan the interview

Before an interview plan carefully how you are going to conduct it and what topics you will cover. Questionnaires and checklists, carefully designed and phrased in advance, will maximize the information-gathering process during the interview. Work from the assumption that people are very busy and don't really want to see you, so pay them the courtesy of being efficient and methodical in your approach to the interview. Techniques of recording such as Mind Maps® and flowcharts can be very useful for gathering information. When collecting facts of a statistical nature always design data collection sheets. A little planning and thought to these sheets will considerably speed up the process of fact collection. It will also make the job of sorting, analysis and interpretation, later on, much easier.

Collect data

It is not sufficient just to flowchart systems and procedures. Quantitative and qualitative data must also be collected – the quantity, quality, cost and time elements of the input, throughput and output factors, including the effectiveness of the systems to the achievement of objectives and standards set. Some systems with the passage of time become an end in themselves rather than contribute towards the achievement of worthwhile goals. Draw up an organization chart if one is not available locally. Make sure that it is accurate and agree it with the staff to ensure that it reflects the actual situation. Is the organization suitable and effective for the achievement of objectives? Is the span of control too small and are there too many reporting levels?

Read any written company policy statements on the area you are studying. They will act as useful guidelines, but remember they are not gospel and may be changed as a result of your findings. You must also take account of external forces which may include political, economic, social, cultural, technological, legal and other factors.

Record as you go

It is important to record all ideas as they occur, facts and information as researched, during the course of your investigation. It is no good convincing yourself that you will think of them when the report writing stage comes. More likely your memory will fail you at this juncture. Remember that 80 per cent of what we hear is forgotten within 24 hours unless we record and review. Your notes are a permanent record for reference and your Mind Maps®, if drawn up carefully, will be an aid to, and form the basis of, the writing and compilation of your findings and report.

Finally, keep your records – Mind Maps®, data collection sheets, layout diagrams, notes, observations and flowcharts – in some systematic order. Set an example. If you are not organized yourself, you can hardly persuade other people to organize themselves. A looseleaf binder with an appropriate indexing and classification system may be useful. Some people like to record their ideas and facts on cards for later grouping, analysis and interpretation. A portable PC might be a very useful tool to record as you go.

Examine

Adopt a critical, questioning and sceptical attitude to each fact, interview and flowchart. Flowcharts of systems and procedures should reflect the actual situation and be complete in themselves. Apply commonsense principles and make sure that your interpretation of the facts is correct and logical. Differentiate between facts, feelings and opinions. Disregard opinions completely and treat feelings with caution. Be aware of any preconceived ideas and biases that you may have and discount them accordingly. If you've solved similar problems before, the same approach might work again. There is no point in reinventing the wheel.

Use techniques such as ratio analysis, decision trees, discounted cash flow, marginal costing, break-even analysis, gap analysis, growth share matrix, directional policy matrix, SWOT analysis and the product life-cycle to help you analyse the data.

Accept nothing at face value. Check out the facts in a rigorous scientific manner. Be attentive to detail in all things. Analysis and synthesis of data is part of the process. There is a systematic approach to analysing data, which covers the Purpose, Person, Place, Sequence and Means.

Purpose

What is done? You have discovered what is done by:

- direct observation
- compiling flowcharts
- asking staff
- interviewing management and supervisory staff
- studying plans, policies and procedure manuals
- studying job descriptions
- studying organization charts.

Why is it done? This is the most important question. If you can't find a satisfactory answer to this, then you need go no further. For example, some office procedures are necessary to meet statutory requirements such as VAT and PAYE returns. Others are necessary to meet control, accounting and audit requirements. Managers need management information systems to help them make good decisions. Sometimes the reason for particular information disappears with the passage of time.

Is it necessary? Question the need for forms, operations, procedures and systems. Question registers. Registers – which are bound books for recording, for example, details of invoices received or customer complaints made – are basically inefficient and usually duplicate information held elsewhere. Question objectives and priorities. Question the need for returns and extra copies. For example, the basic requirement of invoices is one copy for the supplier and one for the company. Are other copies necessary? Always go back to basic issues in this manner. What else might be done and what should be done?

Person

Who does it? Find out who is actually doing the work. Why does that person do it? Has that person special training, ability, experience, education or motivation to do the job? Who else might do it? And who else should do it? Should a higher qualified person do it, or could a less qualified person do the job as well? What are the qualifications and special abilities necessary to do the job? Could all or part of the work be delegated? In reassigning duties to staff or transferring staff to new duties you will need the agreement of the people concerned as well as their manager and possibly their trade union representative. If a job rotation policy is operated which has been agreed with the interested parties, then limited transfer of staff between duties is not difficult.

Place

Where is it done? Why is it done there? It may not be the ideal place for the work. The work may be done in that place because of historical or traditional reasons. Research and question these factors thoroughly. Where else might it be done? Where should it be done? With improved communications and computer networking office work need not necessarily be done in expensive metropolitan areas. It can just as easily be carried out in less expensive locations. Homeworking is also an option these days. Consider the following factors:

- *Environment*. You can't make a silk purse out of a sow's ear. If a building was not originally used and designed for the purpose it now serves, you are obviously very constrained in what you can achieve. An old warehouse may be completely unsuitable for modern transport offloading and storage needs. There may be only one viable solution – build a new warehouse designed with modern needs in mind.

- *Ergonomics*. This is the science of adapting office design and equipment to the employees' needs. Not the other way around, as is often the situation. The office must be suitable for the purpose it serves. Layout and work areas should be designed for comfortable working. Chairs should give maximum comfort and desks should be of a suitable height and design. Anti-glare screens should be installed on personal computers to prevent eye-strain.

- *Lighting*. Lighting should be adequate with no glare. There are minimum technical standards for office lighting and these should be adhered to.

- *Heating and ventilation*. Should be adequate for summer and winter conditions.

- *Colour schemes*. Colour can affect mood and productivity. A little paint can often brighten up the spirits as well as the place.

Sequence

When is it done? Why is it done then? In modern business life, jobs are often determined and deadlines dictated by computer requirements.

The computer has brought order and pressure to the office situation. However, there may only be traditional reasons why a job is done at a particular time. When might it be done? When should it be done? By rearranging work schedules, peaks and troughs in workload at particular times, or during particular days, may be eliminated. Staff can thus be more effectively deployed.

Means

How is it done? Why is it done that way? Systems are often employed – a bit added here and there to meet ad hoc contingencies or legislative requirements, such as VAT. As the organization expands and grows the system needs to adapt and change with it. However, at a certain stage and to cater for the increased workload computerization becomes necessary. How else might it be done? How should it be done? This is where some creative thinking is necessary. Obviously certain jobs can be improved or transferred to machines. There are a whole variety of office machines now available that can improve most types of administrative jobs. E-mail can be used to eliminate paper-based correspondence systems.

Develop alternatives

Develop alternative solutions to the problem, but also consider 'doing nothing'. This is the creative stage of the problem-solving sequence. One source of inspiration should be your own experience. Brainstorming and lateral thinking are well-known methods for producing original ideas. Use a Mind Map® to put down your ideas on paper and to show the relationships and interrelationships between different ideas.

In specialized fields such as financial accounting, management accounting, financial management, management, economics, strategic planning and marketing, there are tried and tested standard procedures, techniques and models for solving problems. For example, in marketing you might use the product life-cycle and Ansoff's matrix. You might also consider positioning, segmentation, niche, marketing mix and pricing strategies for different stages of the product life-cycle.

In management you might consider delegation, improving the span of control, reducing the number of levels in the hierarchy, encouraging team spirit, facilitating empowerment, improving controls, training and development and so on. In management accounting there is break-even analysis, marginal costing and discounted cash flow. In strategic management you could consider organic growth or growth by acquisition. Other strategies might include joint venture, franchising, divestment, corporate venturing or a management buyout.

Question

Apply the questioning approach: Why? What? When? Where? How? Who? The most important word in your vocabulary should be 'Why?' If work does not serve a purpose then it should not be done. Look at the problem from a systems viewpoint. Develop the helicopter approach. Put problems into perspective. See how it relates to the wider issues. What impact will your findings and recommendations, if implemented, have on the section, department and company as a whole? Whereas previous stages are analytical and convergent, this stage is creative and divergent. Be aware of the Pareto Principle or the 80:20 rule – the law of the trivial many and the significant few.

Criteria for alternatives

Pick the best alternative. Questions of feasibility and acceptability must be considered. The theoretical best solution is usually impracticable. So tease out the solution against the stark realities of life – organizational politics, compromises and expediency. Consider the following alternatives:

- *Organization*. The different ways of organizing staff and resources to optimize results. Is the organization structure suitable? Is it a flat or a tall organization? How many levels of management are there? Has it adjusted to the changing needs and culture of the business? Or has it become outdated and in need of overhaul?

- *Systems*. Systems are the oil that run the organization. Could systems be eliminated, modified or improved? What degree of computerization is desirable?

- *Forms*. Are all our forms necessary? Could the design of our forms be improved? Are they user friendly? Have all our forms been standardized? Is there control on the creation of new forms?

- *Office equipment*. Is office equipment introduced as necessary and used to maximum effect? Have we standardized the type of PCs and office equipment that we buy and, if not, why not? Have we standardized the type of software packages in use throughout the company?

- *Method study*. Has everything been done to minimize effort and maximize human efficiency? Have we devised best methods for ongoing repetitive operations?

- *Office layout*. Are our offices laid out to minimize movement and travel? Are chairs comfortable and adaptable to different height requirements? Are our filing systems efficient with fast and easy retrieval? Do we employ the latest telecommunications systems, such as e-mail? Are our offices painted in cheerful colours? Are lighting, heating and ventilation standards adequate?

- *Training*. Are the staff adequately trained to perform their duties efficiently? Poor operating methods leading to poor productivity can be caused by a lack of skills which could be remedied by training.

Develop improvements by:

- eliminating unnecessary forms, operations, procedures and systems
- simplifying forms, operations, procedures and systems

- combining forms, operations, procedures and systems
- rearranging and changing the sequence to eliminate peaks and troughs of work, thereby optimizing the deployment of staff and resources.

Pick the best alternative

Having considered the alternative strategies that the company should pursue, pick the best alternative or combination of alternatives. Obviously there are many alternative solutions to any problem, therefore you should rank alternatives in terms of their importance. Look at the pros and cons of each. Eliminate the impractical and less profitable. Risk and uncertainty should be taken into account. Consider qualitative as well as quantitative outcomes of solutions. The criteria for the best alternative should include cost benefit analysis, practicability and acceptability of the proposed solution. What is the effect on the bottom line result? To be worthwhile the overall profitability, effectiveness and efficiency of the organization should improve.

In choosing the best alternatives use the following:

- *Logical reasoning.* Ask yourself: 'What would a reasonable person do in these circumstances?'

- *Experience.* You may have experience of solving a similar problem before. However, be aware that the circumstances may have changed and that you may have to take this into account.

- *Intuition.* This is a type of third sense, hunch, gut-feeling or premonition that one particular course of action is the right one to take in the circumstances.

- *Experimentation.* A trial run may be possible, but in many cases it is impractical. For example, in product development a prototype may be produced and in marketing test marketing may be employed.

- *Advice.* Seek out other people's advice. They may have had experience of solving a similar problem.

A problem may finally be solved by a combination of factual information, logic, advice, intuition and experience. Where alternatives have been reduced to two which are equal, the choice may be made on a personal preference basis. Remember, a combination of alternatives may be the best solution. In these days of emphasis on participation and team work, group decision making is often employed.

Implement

Accepting and implementing change involves a big selling job. The source of sound suggestions and ideas should be acknowledged and credit given to the staff concerned. The changes must be acceptable to the staff if they have any chance of being implemented. Staff resistance can jeopardize the process. Decide on the options for implementation. An overall plan should be drawn up so that the final installation job runs smoothly and satisfactorily.

The implementation plan

Consider the following factors when compiling your implementation plan:

- *Time schedule.* Allocate your time and human resources to the implementation phases. A simple matrix, bar chart or critical path analysis diagram may help to formalize and crystallize the plan. Nothing elaborate is needed; just something that works for you.

- *Form design.* Take the printing time and cost into account.

- *Office equipment.* Consider special accommodation and furniture for the equipment and layout of the office, and the delivery time of the equipment. Staff may need training in the new equipment.

- *Communications.* Staff must be informed about the whole implementation process and the part they will play in it. Give them an opportunity to express their views, opinions and any queries which they may have. This is very important feedback.

- *Instruction manuals*. Prepare manuals which cover the implementation and ongoing operation of the new system. Seek input from operating staff.

- *Staff training*. Staff may need training in the operation of the new forms, procedures, systems and machines. Allow adequate time and staff resources.

- *Changeover*. You will have to opt for one of the following: direct changeover, pilot run or parallel operation. Be flexible in case things don't run as smoothly as expected.

As part of your plan consider delegation, training and development, improved communication channels, counselling and reorganization. List the types of problems, constraints and obstacles that may be encountered and have to be overcome in practice when you attempt to sell and implement the solution, for example, limited resources of staff and time, staff resistance to change, trade union objections, company policy and so on. When will implementation take place? How will it be done? Who will do it? How much will it cost? Have you drawn up an implementation plan?

What would be the corporate, financial, production, personnel, marketing, organizational, behavioural, customer and competitive implications of implementing the strategy? What contingency plans should you make to overcome likely problems?

Monitor and follow up

Monitor and follow up to see that all the changes as agreed and recommended have in fact been implemented and that they have proved to be as successful as intended and also to learn from problems and shortcomings. The review of failures is an important opportunity for feedback leading to corrective action and improved performance in the future. There should be periodic reviews to see what practical difficulties have been encountered in the operation of the system and what modifications are necessary to rectify any problems.

After a longer period of time a few spot checks might prove useful. In the office system there is a phenomenon which could be called 'drift'. All matter reverts to its original state. Unless properly monitored there is a tendency for staff to drift back into the old ways of doing things and so eventually the situation would be back to square one if not checked.

Summary

- SREDIM is a mnemonic for the scientific approach used in problem solving and stands for Select, Record, Examine, Develop, Implement and Monitor.

- Select is synonymous with the identification of the problem The real problem should be identified and crystallized in writing. Record the facts but differentiate between facts, opinions and assumptions. Mind Maps®, systems flowcharts and other aids may make our recording more meaningful. Examine and challenge the facts collected by systematically determining the purpose, person, place, sequence and means of all work done.

- Develop alternatives. The questioning approach, systems approach and use of the Pareto Principle will all help to develop worthwhile ideas and solutions. Consider organization, systems, communications, forms, computers, method study, office layout and training. Eliminate, simplify, combine and rearrange as appropriate. The best alternative must be worthwhile, feasible and acceptable.

- The implementation phase should be planned carefully. Procedures and systems installed should ensure that savings anticipated have been realized and that changes recommended have been implemented.

4 Creativity

- What is creativity?
- What are the barriers to creativity?
- What are the stages of creativity?
- What is brainstorming?
- What techniques are available to improve creativity?
- How can I use Mind Maps® to become more creative?

What is creativity?

Creativity is creating something that wasn't there before; seeing novel relationships between things, ideas and people. Apart from making something new, creativity can also be changing or combining things in new or novel ways. Creativity is needed throughout a business at strategic, management and operational levels. It should be supported by the chief executive and its importance promulgated throughout all levels of management. Without creativity a firm is unlikely to be innovative and without innovation it is unlikely to be commercially successful.

Specifically creativity is needed in areas of business such as research and development, training and development, management services, product development, strategic planning, marketing, advertising, design and manufacturing. In a quickly changing world new products and technologies are appearing all the time. Apart from new inventions there is continuous improvement on existing products, systems and services. To keep your competitive edge you must at least keep up with the best and more often be better.

Think of the word creative and other words like imaginative, unpredictable, divergent and lateral come to mind. These words convey the message of generating ideas and looking at problems from different perspectives. Creative is the opposite of analytical. Analytical means logical, predictable, convergent and vertical. Conventional education tends to develop our analytical skills. The two types of thinking are inclusive and complementary. Ideally we should be both creative and logical as the circumstances demand.

What are the barriers to creativity?

- *Conformity*. People do not like to be different. They like to be part of the crowd. There are all sorts of pressures on us to be the same. People don't like to think. They like to do the accepted or conventional thing rather than the novel or unusual. Bureaucratic organizational cultures often reward conformity and discourage initiative. Conformity is comforting. Change is traumatic. If managers want to encourage creativity and innovation in organizations they must simplify the bureaucratic machine. Structures may also influence the level of creativity in an organization. Centralized structures generally encourage rigidity and bureaucratic thinking, whereas decentralized structures facilitate creativity and innovative thinking.

- *The one right answer*. All our training and education is left-brained. Our education is largely concerned with language and numbers. We are taught to be logical, convergent and predictable rather than imaginative, creative and lateral. At school we are given the impression that there is one right answer to all problems which resides in the teacher. However, in real life there are many different solutions to most problems and many grey areas and very few people have all the answers.

- *Evaluating too quickly.* Be the angel's advocate rather than the devil's advocate. Write down the ideas. Suspend judgement. Let the ideas flow rather than being critical and dismissive too early and quickly. Let the creative juices flow – time enough to be analytical later. The objective should be to crystallize as many ideas as possible in writing. Quantity rather than quality should be the key at this stage.

- *Afraid to challenge the obvious.* Try to see things from different perspectives. One plus one is not always two. It may be eleven, a cross, a T and so on. Use your imagination for the different possibilities. A questioning approach is essential to unearth issues and see novel relationships that have not been thought of before.

- *The self-imposed barrier.* Sometimes barriers are traditional and psychological rather than real. For many years it was thought impossible to run a mile in less than 4 minutes. Then Roger Bannister came along and the psychological barrier was broken. Numerous runners subsequently broke the barrier.

- *In fear of looking a fool.* Some people are often inhibited to suggest ideas because they fear a negative reaction or that they will be held up to ridicule. This may be the position in a group of staff, peers and managers. Staff are afraid to offer ideas in front of their managers in case they are thought to be foolish. On the other hand, managers are reluctant to make suggestions in case they look foolish in front of their staff.

Killers of creativity

Creativity killers in organizations include:

> 'It's a good idea, but it won't work here.'
> 'We tried that before.'
> 'It will upset the manager.'
> 'It will probably cost too much.'
> 'It won't travel.'

'There are too many complications.'
'Competitors will copy our idea quickly.'
'It's against company policy.'
'Yes but' is a famous killer phrase and denotes a negative mind set. Why not substitute 'Yes and' which suggests opening up possibilities and a positive mind set?

These are just some of the typical statements that stultify creativity and personal initiative in an organization. The 'not invented here' syndrome also spells the death knell of many a good idea before it has time to germinate. Some departments are not prepared to entertain good ideas from other departments or sources relating to their area. Similarly, some managers are not prepared to consider ideas from their staff.

The five stages of creativity

The five stages of creativity are: preparation, effort, incubation, insight and evaluation. They use a combination of left-brain logical skills and right-brain imaginative skills.

- *Preparation*. Preparation includes being in the right mood or frame of mind to think deeply about the problem in hand. A problem must become part of you. You must sleep with it, eat with it and play with it. You must think about it continually. Try and imagine looking at it from as many different viewpoints as possible. See the problems from above and below. View them from the side. Let the problem brew in your mind. Redefine the problem using the words 'how to'. At this stage too you must read widely. To promote creativity you must diversify your interests and reading in order to generate divergent views. Collect all information and relevant facts about the problem, including field and desk research. Consult your staff to get fresh and different viewpoints.

- *Effort*. Develop and record all ideas and alternatives. Use the technique of brainstorming to generate ideas. Brainstorming is a type of group discussion process in which members of the group are encouraged in a helpful and uncritical manner to generate as many imaginative and creative ideas and suggestions as possible within a defined period of time, under a chairman. These ideas are recorded for subsequent evaluation and criticism by a group leader. The initial emphasis is on quantity rather than quality, so suspend judgement. Seemingly unusual ideas may form the germ of perfectly practicable solutions. Where staff are not available conduct individual brainstorming sessions with the aid of Mind Maps®. The Mind Maps® can be added to and developed as you pick up further ideas through reading, research, observation, reflection, watching television, and consulting with operational and specialist staff.

- *Incubation*. Mull over the problem in your mind. Don't ignore your intuition or sixth sense as gut feelings sometimes have practical validity. There are plenty of examples of successful people following their gut feelings with great determination and persistence against much opposition and winning in the end. Many management decisions are based on experience and judgement, which is probably a nicer way of saying gut feeling. What are the pros and cons of each alternative? Which or what combination of alternatives is the best? Then put it aside and think of other issues. Sleep on it. Your subconscious will now be working on the problem.

- *Insight*. The 'Eureka' feeling. A sudden flash of illumination and a release of tension when the problem has been solved.

- *Evaluation*. Test the idea. Does it work? Discard ideas that are too costly, unacceptable, inappropriate or unethical. Tease out the solution against the stark realities of life – organizational politics, cost, compromises and expediency.

Brainstorming

The stages of brainstorming are: suspend judgement, freewheel, generate quantity of ideas and cross-fertilize. Generally you need to separate idea production from idea evaluation. Judgement is postponed, not abandoned. Later on the ideas will be subjected to critical analysis. It's good practice to have the brainstorming group as varied as possible. Your group could include, inter alia, an accountant, engineer, marketing person and personnel manager. A mix of backgrounds and personalities will help the group to synergize and consider the problem from different perspectives.

Suspend judgement

The emphasis is on the generation of ideas, so suspend your judgement. Even though you know the idea is very silly and all the reasons why it won't work, nevertheless you must keep quiet. In fact the 'wildest idea' technique is sometimes used as a stimulant when ideas are beginning to dry up. Put your critical faculties into neutral gear. Freewheel the ideas. Let them flow. One idea may trigger off new ideas or novel relationships. At this stage you are looking for quantity of ideas rather than quality. Some ideas can be linked, associated or combined with others to give new ideas. It may be useful to keep the laws of association in mind here: contiguity, similarity and contrast. What do the ideas remind you of? What are opposite ideas? What are the related ideas and issues? The different people in the group with different backgrounds, experience and knowledge will cross-fertilize causing a synergy of ideas.

Brainstorming has been used in business in work simplification and cost reduction programmes and has achieved significant savings. Quality circles is a modern application of the idea. Mind Maps® are a very useful technique for brainstorming on an individual basis – individuals can produce more and better ideas than a group.

Creativity and Mind Maps®

Mind mapping helps us pull information together in such a way that it encourages making new connections. It concentrates our thoughts quickly into the insight stage of creativity. The structure of Mind Maps® helps to generate ideas, integrate information and provide synthesis, links, combinations, relationships and associations between ideas. Surveys of creative thinking have emphasized the importance of encouraging an initial right-brain visualization, an intuitive solution, which can then be evaluated logically by the left brain. Visual images appear to be a main communication medium of the right brain. Therefore, if the essence of a problem can be shown visually, as on a Mind Map®, the creative capacities of the right brain can be more accessed in problem solving. Mind Maps® encourage extrapolation of ideas and facilitate the perception of unusual relationships between ideas which are otherwise not easily seen.

Mind Maps® and genius

Buzan, the inventor of Mind Maps®, maintains that they enhance creativity. To support this claim he draws on the work of past geniuses, whose notebooks display the characteristics of Mind Maps® such as non-linearity and images. For example, Leonardo da Vinci was as much scientist as artist, an engineer and architect, as well as sculptor and painter. His science notebooks, in addition to the words and analysis, contain marvellous drawings of nature and of the human anatomy. The notebooks of many other artists similarly reveal concise analytic thinking, linked with deep insight and aesthetic appreciation.

Einstein, as well as being the most famous scientist, was also an accomplished violinist and painter. He thus had both scientific and artistic skills. The use of images and drawings by the great geniuses would seem to support the idea of the value of using the non-linear, spatial approach and visualization, images, codes and symbols, in conjunction with words in Mind Maps®.

Mind Maps® are ideally suited to creative thinking because they require all the skills commonly associated with creativity, especially imagination, association and integration of ideas and flexibility. The open-ended nature of the structure of Mind Maps® facilitates the addition of new ideas, relationships and connections. Thus the material is never locked into a final format – you can always expand and restructure your knowledge. In fact, their open-ended nature actively encourages the creation of new ideas, relationships and connections. Mind Maps® have been well received by educators and business people in Europe. They help them develop a far greater number of creative ideas than traditional list making and outlining.

Benefits of Mind Maps®

There are many benefits of using Mind Maps® for idea generation, including the following:

- They are easy to learn, teach and use.
- They are capable of generating a large number of ideas quickly.
- They are an efficient way of recording, processing and relating ideas.
- They are very flexible. It is easy to add ideas.
- They are faster than linear note-taking.
- They give an overview of the problem and a better understanding of the issues involved.
- The brain abhors a vacuum. The open-ended structure of Mind Maps® facilitates the creation, association, connection and interconnection of ideas.
- They facilitate review and recall.
- Unlike brainstorming, they can be done on an individual as well as on a group basis.
- With the right technique, such as Mind Maps®, people can be as creative individually as in a group.

Some techniques for stimulating creativity

The following techniques are helpful in making people more creative:

- *Metaphor*. Metaphorical thinking is the ability to link two different things by recognizing that in some way they share a common trait or show a common principle; for example, a revolution is compared to a volcano (a build-up of pressure leading to an explosion) and electricity is compared to water flowing through pipes. The ability to play with ideas and concepts is basic to problem solving and creativity. Metaphor allows this type of play to occur. So making comparisons between problems in business and in biology, science and so on may help to unlock solutions.

- *Reverse brainstorming*. This is a negative approach to brainstorming. Instead of asking 'In how many ways can we ...?' this technique asks 'In how many ways can this idea fail?' It is a good way to tease out problems in advance so that potential solutions can be thought through. Play the devil's advocate with your proposals and anticipate objections so that you are prepared with the appropriate answers – very useful when you are presenting proposals to your boss for discussion as a way of anticipating flaws in your argument. Preparation with anticipation is the key to success.

- *Forced relationships*. If you combine two objects or ideas, what will be the outcome? This technique may be useful in many areas including new product development; for example, the combination of a video cassette recorder with a television for a new type of equipment. Another example might be combining a desk and a chair which is a common piece of furniture in modern colleges.

- *Checklists*. Used in many areas including management services, marketing and design. They prevent you from overlooking key aspects of the problem. One such list is Osborn's Generalized Checklist, by Alex F. Osborn, the inventor of brainstorming, which provides the following headings:

– Put to other uses?
– Adapt?
– Modify?
– Magnify?
– Minify?
– Substitute?
– Rearrange?
– Reverse?
– Combine?

A simplified version, which may help you to remember the rather cumbersome list above, can be recalled by the mnemonic ROMANCES:

Reverse (rearrange)
One for another (substitute)
Modify (magnify, minify)
Adapt
New uses
Combine
Eliminate
Simplify

Beware. Checklists as well as encouraging creativity may in fact inhibit other lines of enquiry.

- *Attribute listing*. List the main characteristics of an idea or object. Examine each to see if it can be improved or changed. Value analysis has a similar approach. Products can be improved by this technique. Each aspect of the product is examined in every way. Unnecessary parts or features are eliminated for greater efficiency and cost reduction. Reverse engineering, where a company takes a competitor's product and disassembles it to see if it could be improved in any way, is another application of this idea.

- *Serendipity*. Serendipity is the discovery of things by happy accident or chance, such as Fleming is purported to have done with penicillin. However, it is said that discovery favours the prepared mind and in fact many discoveries have been made by people who were obsessed by and immersed in their subjects and after much patient work and research. They were 'overnight success' stories after many years' hard work and struggle.

- *Stimuli*. Pick a word at random from a dictionary and through metaphorical thinking relate it to the problem at hand. Sometimes the juxtaposition of the word with the problem will trigger off novel ideas and associations. If you're stuck for ideas, this approach may unlock the process.

- *Visual thinking*. Use graphs, charts, diagrams, models and Mind Maps® to represent your ideas visually. They will help to give you an overview and see relationships previously not clear and may also help you to solve problems and generate ideas. A physical representation, such as a prototype model which can be experimented upon, will help you to concentrate on the problem by involving all the senses.

- *Fantasy*. Research in problem solving and creativity shows that creative adults use fantasy for a number of purposes. Fantasy opens up other worlds. In your imagination you create your own realities unfettered by time and space. Within it you travel to India and shrink to the size of an atom to explore microscopic worlds. The idea of becoming something in order to understand it better may be applied to any problem. You can become anything the mind can think of. Albert Einstein's fantasy of himself riding a beam of sunlight played an important part in the discovery of the theory of relativity.

- *Morphological analysis*. Look at all the possible variations in a problem and try to combine them in new and novel ways. Morphological analysis is often drawn in the form of a matrix. It is a method of exploring opportunities rather than solving specific problems; for example, a packaging problem might have three dimensions – the shape of the package, the packaging material and the content of the package. Potential applications include new product development, exploring the use of different raw materials, considering the development of new market segments for your products and services, developing different promotion strategies, different distribution strategies, determining competitive advantage and location selection.

- *Suggestion schemes.* Companies may set up suggestion schemes to encourage staff to make improvements related to their work. Sometimes managers may publicize current problems and offer prizes for solutions which can be implemented with cost savings. Small money incentives may be awarded for ideas which are worth implementing. A centralized suggestion committee may be set up to adjudicate and make awards. Remember that a suggestion scheme will need continuous senior management support if it is to live beyond the razzmatazz of the launch.

- *Treat problems as potential opportunities.* Create a culture in which problems are examined for sources of opportunities. This positive approach to problem solving will create imaginative solutions.

- *SWOT analysis.* This is a technique used in strategic planning and stands for **S**trengths, **W**eaknesses, **O**pportunities and **T**hreats. A threat or weakness, in fact, is often a matter of attitude or perspective. A more positive approach might be to consider how to turn the threat into an opportunity.

- *Force field analysis.* A technique to find out what impact a proposed solution is likely to have during implementation. Solutions are subject to a myriad of forces, some supportive called driving forces, and some unhelpful and constraining called restraining forces. A situation which is to be changed is regarded as a balance of forces working in opposite directions – resisting forces and driving forces. The situation can be changed in two ways:
  – by increasing the strength of the driving forces or
  – by removing or decreasing the resisting forces.
  An increase in the driving forces is likely to increase tension and conflict. Permanent change is facilitated through the reduction or elimination of the resisting forces. This has the effect of 'unfreezing' the situation, and allowing movement to a new, changed situation. The final step is to 'freeze' the situation in its new, changed state. For example, when considering the introduction of an open learning centre in an organization the driving forces might include:

– competition means that the company must make its training more cost effective
– the need for employee training in information technology skills
– the need to decentralize training and make it available to all employees
– employee desire for empowerment in their own training and development
– the support of board room management.

The restraining forces might include:

– company culture is bureaucratic and resists any change
– managers are sceptical about open learning
– trainers see open learning as a threat to their jobs
– the initial capital investment is high and the return seen as uncertain or difficult to quantify
– no existing tradition or experience in the company in computer-based training.

The decision maker can now use the analysis to evaluate how the restraining factors can be removed or reduced and how to reinforce the driving forces.

- *Quality circle.* A quality circle is an employee discussion group, usually of production operatives under the guidance of a specially trained group leader. Circles meet periodically to consider, analyse and resolve quality and production control difficulties. They are an institutionalized and participative mechanism for diagnosing and solving productivity and quality problems. Although developed by an American, Dr W.E. Deming, they are now mostly associated with Japanese industry where they have been extensively and successfully adapted.

Summary

- Creativity is creating something that wasn't there before; seeing novel relationships between things, ideas and people. The barriers to creativity include:

- conformity
- the one right answer
- evaluating too quickly
- afraid to challenge the obvious
- the self-imposed barrier and
- in fear of looking a fool.

- The five stages of creativity are:
  - preparation
  - effort
  - incubation
  - insight and
  - evaluation.

- Brainstorming can be used by groups to generate ideas. Some techniques for improving creativity were discussed including:
  - metaphor
  - reverse brainstorming
  - forced relationships
  - checklists
  - attribute listing
  - serendipity
  - SWOT analysis and
  - visual thinking.

- On an individual basis Mind Maps® are a good way to foster creativity.

Chapter 4 Use this page to draw your own Mind Map® of this chapter

5 Effective memory

- What are the laws of remembering?
- How can I improve my memory?
- What is the PLAN system of memory?
- How can I use mnemonics to improve my recall?
- What is the systematic approach to applying memory to exam topics?

General principles

The average person uses only 10 per cent of his normal capacity. In case this 'regularly' quoted statistic is not thought provoking enough, it is now felt that you are not using even 1 per cent of your brain's potential. There is obviously plenty of room for improvement! Memory is a very important skill in everyday life and especially when studying. To be successful in work you need to build up an adequate data base of knowledge in your discipline and be familiar with the functional expertise of other departments. Most people know very little about how their memory works. Very few people receive any training on memory techniques which can enhance their ability to recall information.

This chapter recommends a few practical tips that will help you to remember things better, especially in the area that concerns you most – work and study! It will show you how to use mnemonics as vehicles for organizing key points on memory and will illustrate how these devices can be used to help you recall information instantly! A knowledge of the laws of memory and, of course, use of that knowledge can help you utilize some of the spare capacity of your brain. The three laws of memory and the first mnemonic are IMPRESSION, REPETITION and ASSOCIATION (IRA).

Impression

Form a deep vivid impression of what you want to remember. To do this you must concentrate and focus your attention on the material you are studying. Use your powers of observation. A camera will not take good pictures in poor lighting conditions. Similarly, your mind will not register and remember impressions when there are inconsistencies in your mental ideas of a subject.

Impression is, therefore, the ability to imagine or picture what you want to remember in your mind's eye. Reading is a left-brain function. This is the side of the brain which specializes in logic, words, numbers and language. To make your reading more memorable you must also use the righthand side of the brain which specializes in creativity, imagination, colour and daydreaming. So when you're reading try and live and visualize the experience. You may find this difficult at first, nevertheless the very fact that you are trying will improve your concentration and thus help you remember information better.

External impressions such as sight, sound, smell, touch and taste are formed by keeping your eyes open, observing and actively involving yourself in the world about you. Internal impressions such as interest, understanding and attention are formed by closing your eyes, visualizing and reflecting on your experience. For example, when trying to recall a section of a book you could visualize the key points in your mind's eye or better still write them down.

Employ all your senses

Employ all your different senses. Visual for pages, diagrams and pictures. Auditory for paraphrasing, recitation and reading aloud. Kinaesthetic (the muscles used in writing and the sensations felt by trying to relive the experiences in your imagination) for note-taking and visualization. Forming mental images or drawing diagrams or flowcharts of key points of material will help you really understand them. Drawing or note-taking uses the left or verbal side of the brain. Using imagination draws on the right or visual side of your brain. Thus your ability to recall the information is more than doubled.

Forming mental images or drawing diagrams or flowcharts of work systems will help you to fully understand and imprint the information on your mind. Some educationalists argue that this is effective because it involves the left (logic) and right (creative) hemispheres of the brain. On the other hand, drawing diagrams or flowcharts brings the right or creative side of the brain into action. Thus your chances of understanding and recalling the information are multiplied.

Live the experiences by visualizing the use of as many of the senses as possible. For example, when reading company law picture the process involved when registering a limited company. Imagine yourself completing the necessary documentation. Sense the feel of the paper. Picture the inside of Companies House and the bureaucratic hassle you might go through to finalize the registration. To make the process stand out in your mind even more, imagine you have a ferocious argument with the official at Companies House about some aspect of the procedure. Involving the limbic system or emotions is a great way of enhancing learning.

Discussion groups

Discussion and learning groups are a useful adjunct to training and development. After attending a course discuss it with a fellow participant. The discussion will give you different perspectives on the course while holding your concentration and stimulating your mind. It also brings variety into the learning approach. Doing a course in an open learning centre can be a solitary experience. Why not discuss the programme with someone who has already completed the course?

Develop an interest in your job for better learning and recall. Take an interest in the work of the other departments that you deal with. Read around your discipline and also take notice of the functional expertise of the other departments. This will provide context and interest for your own job. At the very least read your professional journal and the business pages in the newspapers. Interest creates motivation and counteracts boredom. Integrate what you want to remember into your everyday activities by applying ideas to your job. Information is forgotten quickly if it is not actively used.

The 'MUSE principle'

If you dramatize, personalize and emotionalize something you are more likely to remember it. Therefore put Movement, Unusualness, Slapstick and Exaggeration into your mental images. Remember the mnemonic MUSE (in mythology a Muse was one of the nine goddesses inspiring learning and the arts) principle for more effective recall.

Information is retained better if it answers a question. Put down in a Mind Map® the amount of knowledge that you already have on the topic and the answers to the questions that you seek. This is the knowledge gap. This exercise creates the proper mental set or attitude for learning as memory abhors a vacuum. Remember the Kipling verse:

> I keep six honest serving-men
> (They taught me all I knew);
> Their names are What and Why and When
> And How and Where and Who.

Commit this verse to memory.

The three Rs of memory

The three Rs of memory are RECEPTION, RETENTION and RECALL. GIGO is a well-known mnemonic used in computer circles – 'garbage in, garbage out'. The same idea can be used in learning and memory. Obviously, to remember something you must register it on your imagination and transfer it from your short-term to your long-term memory.

Constantly reflecting and thinking about your subject will help this process to take place. It will ensure that the information is retained in your long-term memory. What you are doing, of course, is overlearning the information. Recall is the ability to retrieve information when needed. When trying to recall from written sources use your vivid imagination. Written words in themselves are dead. The author had pictures in his head before writing the words and you must translate those words back into pictures. This translation of words into pictures will imprint the information on your imagination.

Repetition

The second law of memory is repetition. Muslim students memorize the Koran – a book as long as the New Testament – by repetition. Repetition is how we learnt the number tables at school and also how we learnt the alphabet. Psychologists call this overlearning. The material is embedded in our long-term memory. This is the approach to adopt when learning key points and important definitions, say, for that critical presentation or when preparing for that vital professional exam. Rote learning is not recommended except in these particular instances. Build up your database of key points and concepts in your topic and you can expand on these yourself. When using the repetition technique keep the following points in mind:

> Space out your repetition for better recall. Go over it a few times, then drop it; come back later and go over it again. Reviewing at intervals in this manner, will help you memorize in about half the time it takes at one sitting. Review is particularly important after 24 hours and less frequently thereafter. Remember we forget 50 per cent of what we read immediately, 80 per cent within 24 hours, and about 90 per cent within 48 hours, unless we review.

Systematic review plan

Working to a systematic review plan, you would review matter after 10 minutes, 1 day, 1 week, 1 month, 4 months and frequently coming up towards the examination. Keep a review file. Imagine you take some notes on 1 January. Do review 1 on 1 January. Date your notes for the first review. In this case it will be on 2 January, i.e. 24 hours later. Therefore, put 2 January at the top of your notes. Review 3 will be on 9 January. Review 4 will be on 4 February. Review 5 will be on 9 June. This will put the key points into your long-term memory. Each day check the date on each page of your notes. Notes with today's date on them should be reviewed now and then forward dated for the next review. In general, review from Mind Maps® and cue cards when preparing for presentations. In addition, when revising for exams, review questions at the end of chapters, past exam questions and answers, lecturer's comments and examiner's reports. In the work context there is no substitute for an efficient filing system and a good diary as memory aids.

Discuss the content of a business book or report with a colleague after reading it and thereby reinforce your memory of it. When reading imagine that you will be called on to give a presentation on the topic. This has the marvellous effect of focusing the mind on the topic. On a lower key, imagine that you will be required to explain it to your manager or colleague after reading it.

Alternate periods of reading and recall

For technical matter alternate your periods of reading and recall. Recall at the end of each section and again at the end of each chapter. Paraphrase the author's thoughts in your own words. Recalling constantly aids reading comprehension and monitors progress. The first time you do this write down the points you can recall. Compare them with the text and fill in the gaps. Use these notes to compile your Mind Maps® of key points, particularly if you are preparing for a presentation. When reading difficult technical reports or business books which are important for you to remember, spend 50 per cent of your time recalling. Continuous feedback through recall is essential for effective memory.

Think about your subject during spare moments of the day, for example, while walking along the street, waiting for a bus or commuting to and from work. Use cue cards for this purpose. The famous American psychologist William James said: 'the one who thinks over his experiences most and weaves them into systematic relations with each other will be the one with the best memory'.

Psychologists reckon we should spend as much as 50 per cent of our time recalling information. Don't just verbalize the recall, write it down. Better still, draw a Mind Map® of the key points. This is a left-brain activity. To make it more memorable, reflect on the topic and actively associate information to make it unique and outstanding. Picture the information in your mind's eye. This process uses the right side of your brain.

Association

The third law of memory is association – linking new information with knowledge and experience that you already have. Relate your professional studies to your work and try to integrate them with your everyday life experience. Apply the questioning technique to build up the necessary links and to engrave the subject-matter on your memory. Why is this so? How is this so? When is it so? Where is it so? Who said it? What else could be deduced? The brain is the only organ that expands through use. The more it is used, the more memory associations are formed. The more associations are formed, the easier it is to remember previously acquired information, and also to form new associations.

The three laws of association

There are three laws of association which you may find useful. The first is the law of similarity, which states that two ideas may be associated if they resemble each other. For example, people with the same name. The second law of association is the law of contrast, which states that two ideas may be associated if they contrast with each other. For example, tall and short, day and night. These laws suggest that comparing and contrasting ideas is a very effective way of learning information. The third law is the law of contiguity, which states that two ideas may be associated if they have occurred together. For example, if two important events happened on the same or near enough dates, one may be recalled by reference to the other. We all know that the First World War started in 1914. Frederick Winslow Taylor, the 'Father of Scientific Management' died the following year in 1915. Connect the two events and you now have a way of recalling the date of Taylor's death.

Information is retained better if obtained in answer to a question. This creates active learning and the proper mental set. Put down in Mind Map® form the knowledge you know already about the topic and the questions that you want answered. Develop an interest in the subject as this will improve your ability to learn and recall. Integrate what you want to remember into everyday activities. Things are forgotten through disuse.

People tend to have better recall of items which are linked, categorized and conceptually related in some way. Mind Maps® will help you to do this. Research shows that organized information can be learnt four times faster than information which is not. Reading strategies that pay attention to individual ideas and to how they are organized and related produce better recall. There are three techniques for mental organization. First, sequencing – putting items into chronological or alphabetical order. Secondly, categorizing – grouping items according to some common characteristic such as colour, shape or other similarity. Thirdly, relational imagery – organizing items round a theme such as work, holidays, Christmas etc. People remember things better in relation to a particular context. Contextual features become associated with material being learned, and serve as cues for recall.

Short-term memory

Short-term memory (STM) is the amount of information a person can recognize and recall after a single presentation without practice. STM decays rapidly without rehearsal, with estimates ranging up to 18 seconds duration. Like long-term memory, interference seems to be the prime cause of forgetting in STM.

The capacity of STM is between 5 and 9 items of information. However, its capacity can be extended if the material is grouped. For example, a memory span of 7 letters can be increased to 35 if the letters form seven five-letter words. Therefore, 'chunk' the learning points into related groups of between 5 and 9 items. The isolated words such as mnemonics can be easily memorized if you are astute enough to organize them into a meaningful sentence or a little story. Whole areas of a topic can therefore be recalled quite easily. In memorizing, say, a definition, the central part requires more attention than the two extremes. So make the central part unique and outstanding and you will remember it better.

Use the SQ3R method – survey, question, read, recall and review. Use this method when reading instead of the '3R' approach, i.e. read, read and re-read. SQ3R is a telescopic approach where you first learn a broad outline followed by successive layers of detail. The survey, question part of this formula gives you the framework and provides hooks to link and associate information as you read.

Memory and understanding

MUD is a mnemonic for Memory, Understanding and Doing. Obviously if you want to remember something you should understand it. Memory is but one of the ingredients of effective learning. Memorizing involves association, repetition, review, paraphrasing and self-testing. Understanding involves questioning, comparing, contrasting, analysis, synthesis and problem solving. Doing involves some sort of physical activity with practice sessions to achieve perfection. So organize your material, be thorough and make sure that you understand what you are committing to memory.

The greater our existing knowledge, the greater our insight, understanding and ability to make meaningful associations. Wide and extensive reading will provide a sound foundation on which additional knowledge can be built. Pay attention to meanings and make extensive use of associations. Look for similarities, contrasts, advantages and disadvantages and relate everything you can to your fund of knowledge and experience. Use the SQ3R system for better understanding, retention and recall.

Detailed memory laws – FIBRES

Brain cells, when viewed under a microscope, look like tiny octopuses with tentacles or fibres emanating from them. This should help you link the mnemonic FIBRES with memory. FIBRES is an elaboration of the three basic laws discussed in the foregoing paragraphs – Frequency, Intensity, Belonging, Recency, Effect (Pygmalion) and Stand out (unique and outstanding).

Frequency

Frequency means exactly the same as repetition. The more often you learn something the better it is understood. One of the most startling discoveries is that we forget 80 per cent of what we read within 24 hours unless we review. This highlights the importance of reviewing critical information within 24 hours and thereafter working to a systematic review plan, if retaining information is important to our careers. The best way to commit a verse to memory is by the progressive part method. The learner adds a new line while continuing to rehearse the other lines. For example, learn line one then learn lines one and two. When you have memorized lines one and two you then tackle lines one, two and three, and so on. Such a procedure ensures:

- that your short-term memory is not overloaded
- the practice and retention of earlier lines, otherwise forgotten through interference.

The progressive part method should be combined with the whole method for best results. In other words, obtain an overview of the material first before using the Progressive Part Method. Belonging, or the 'whole method', is the psychological phenomenon of the mind's preference to deal in the larger natural systems. This is the concept behind the SQ3R system. Build up a framework of the area to be learned and develop it as time progresses. For your next presentation use the progressive part method to learn that verse or quotation and impress your manager and colleagues with your remarkable memory.

Intensity

Intensity, motivation, interest and confidence are all interlinked. Each reinforces the other. The more success you have, the more confident and motivated you become. Similarly, the more enthusiastic you are about a topic the better your recall. For example, a schoolboy may be thought to be stupid and indifferent at studies and yet may have an amazing capacity to recall all the players in his favourite football team, what matches they won and who scored the vital goals. The reason for this, of course, is that soccer has caught his imagination and interest. In reality it is hard to have an intense interest in all aspects of your company, nevertheless be aware of this factor and try and build up enthusiasm and interest for the different functional areas. Develop intense powers of attention and concentration to memorize and learn effectively.

Belonging

Belonging is sometimes called the 'Holistic' method. In management we have the helicopter factor and this is similar. The mind likes to have an overview of a topic before it starts filling in the details. Just as we tackle a jigsaw puzzle. We look at the illustration and then start from the outer edges and work our way inwards. We are using a telescopic approach, going from less detail to more detail. Psychologists call this the 'Gestalt' approach. Mind Maps® are an application of this idea.

Recency/Primacy

Recency means we remember better what we did last, that is, most recently. We forget 50 per cent immediately of what we read and 80 per cent within 24 hours unless we review. Primacy means we remember better what we did first rather than what came subsequently. We remember our first day at school, our first day at work, our first love affair etc. This is the novelty concept and the reason why as a child you learnt so well. Things are impressed on your memory when they are new and novel. So when you are reading a business book for the first time consciously make as much use of the novelty concept as possible. The recency/primacy principle suggests the more starts and finishes in a study period the better. Of course, after each reading period take a five-minute break.

To maintain your level of concentration keep your study sessions to one hour's duration or less, with short rests in-between for review and consolidation of information. Psychologists have found that immediately after you have learnt something is the time when your memory for it is best. This is called the 'reminiscence effect'. Frequent breaks allow you to take advantage of it.

The Pygmalion effect

Educationalists have found that praise produces greater effort than criticism. A little praise now and again will reinforce your motivation to succeed. By the way, don't wait around for other people to praise you. Self-stroking or praising yourself is a type of autosuggestion and is almost as effective. It builds up your self-esteem and powers of positive thinking. The Pygmalion effect suggests that staff live up to their manager's expectations of them. If you have a manager who treats you as an intelligent, mature and able person and sets you high standards of performance you are likely to live up to that manager's expectations. This is a type of 'self-fulfilling prophecy' and McGregor's management 'Theory Y' philosophy in action.

Feelings of competition often intensify the work effort. This phenomenon is well known to training managers who use the case study method to involve participants competitively and imaginatively in the learning process. Remember, it might be more productive to organize employees in project groups or teams.

The Von Restorff effect

In psychology the unique or outstanding idea is called the Von Restorff effect. If you want to recall something, make it unique and outstanding. Remember the MUSE principle? MUSE is a mnemonic for Movement, Unusualness, Slapstick and Exaggeration. In other words, if you want to remember something, visualize it in an unusual context, using vivid imagination, colour, exaggeration and humour. This will make the information more memorable.

The 'PLAN' system of memory

PLAN is a mnemonic for the main systems of memory:

> **P**lace system
> **L**ink system
> **A**lphabet system
> **N**umber rhyme, number shape and number phonetic systems.

Place system

The Place system is also called the method of loci or room system and was used by the Greeks and Romans in ancient times. In those days oratory was a highly prized skill and the ability to address an audience for hours without the use of notes was highly respected. In more modern times, 'S' a famous mnemonist used three basic processes, usually in combination, for remembering verbal information: the first was to use rich visual images to represent information; the second was to use well-known locations, such as stops on a familiar street, to place the images mentally for later retrieval; and the third was to create a story with appropriate images to retrieve the information.

The basic idea of the Place system is to use the items of furniture in each room in your home as hooks to associate or link things to. The hooks might be door, lamp, window, clock, chair, table, plant, TV, cabinet and fireplace. Associate the items you want to remember with these links. Then, when you want to remember them, take a mental walk around your house picking off the items as you go.

It is easier to associate items with familiar pegs, hence the advantage of the room system. It is also expandable in relation to the number of rooms and items in each room in your home. The pegs can also be items you encounter on a familiar walk or car journey. You may have to use concrete words for abstract items – for example, justice, liberty and fraternity. To remember these just think of a judge, the Statue of Liberty and a group of your relatives who have turned up unexpectedly. Visualize the judge sitting on your favourite fireside chair, the Statue of Liberty on top of the TV and your relatives sitting on the sofa. Use the MUSE principle to imprint the items on your memory – Movement, Unusualness, Slapstick and Exaggeration. When next making a presentation, why not use this approach or the following methods to commit information to memory?

Link system

The Link system uses your powers of vivid imagination to associate items together in sequence. Again use the MUSE principle. In other words, see things in an action-related context; larger than life; millions of them; in a humorous situation and in colour. For example, say you want to remember dog, television, pencil and apple. Picture the dog devouring the TV, the TV with pencils stuck out of the screen and apples being knifed with pencils. The more vivid and unusual the association the better you'll recall it.

Alphabet system

In your early school days you committed to memory the 26 letters of the alphabet. This means that you have 26 hooks for associating things to. The idea here is to invent words to represent each letter of the alphabet and commit them to long-term memory. For example, A might be axe, B might be bee, C might be sea, D might be deed and so on. If you want to remember 26 items you link or associate them with these ready-made hooks.

Number systems

- *Number rhyme.* The number rhyme is a well-known memory system used in scores of memory books: 1 is gun, 2 is shoe, 3 is tree, 4 is door, 5 is hive, 6 is sticks, 7 is heaven, 8 is gate, 9 is wine, 10 is hen, 11 is a soccer team and 12 is a shelve. The same principle, of associating items you want to remember with these easily recallable hooks, is used.

- *Number shape.* The number shape is based on the idea of animated digits. The number 1 here could be a pole, 2 is a swan, 3 is a butterfly, 4 is a sailing boat, 5 is a sickle, 6 is a snake, 7 is the bow of a ship, 8 is an hourglass, 9 is a walking stick and 10 is a bat and ball. These could be used as hooks or could be substituted for numbers. To recall 26 you could visualize a swan devouring a snake.

- *Number phonetic system.* This is a fairly complex system and takes some time to master. It involves linking the numbers 1 to 0 with groups of consonants whose shape resembles the numbers:
  1 = t or d (t has one downstroke)
  2 = n (n has two downstrokes)

3 = m (m has three downstrokes)
4 = r (r is the last letter in the word four)
5 = l (the Roman numeral for 50 is L)
6 = j, sh, ch, soft g (j is almost a mirror image of 6)
7 = k, hard c, hard g (a k can be formed from a pair of 7s)
8 = f, v, ph (hand-written f is somewhat like an 8)
9 = p, b (p is a mirror image of a 9)
0 = s, z, soft c (the word zero begins with the z sound).

You can use this system in two ways. You can invent a series of hooks based on the consonants and use them as permanent memory hooks to link things to, for example: 1 might be 'tie', 2 is Noah, 3 is ma, 4 is rye, 5 is law, 6 is shoe, 7 is cow, 8 is ivy, 9 is pea, 10 is toes (you have ten toes). Of course, you can expand this system ad infinitum.

The second way of using this method is to recall numbers. Suppose the number of your friend's house is 74 and you want to commit this to long-term memory. You think of the word 'car' for 74 (c is 7 and r is 4 and you can ignore the vowel under the phonetic system). So you visualize your friend's car on the roof of his house. To remember that Columbus discovered America in 1492, code the number 1 as t, 4 as r, 9 as b, and 2 as n. This converts to TRBN. Add the appropriate vowels and this becomes TURBAN. Now link 'turban' to Columbus (imagine him wearing a turban) and you have a device for remembering the date. Another way to remember this is through the rhyme 'In fourteen hundred and ninety-two, Columbus sailed the ocean blue'.

You won't learn to drive a car by reading a book. Similarly, it takes considerable time, patience and practice to become proficient in the PLAN system of memory. Nevertheless, your efforts will be more than adequately rewarded by the development of an outstanding memory in your area of expertise. Nothing worthwhile is easy to learn and master. So start now, practise and persevere.

Making memory mnemonics

Mnemonics have been used throughout this book and they are very useful for jogging memory. Don't overdo them, however, or you'll have a job trying to remember the mnemonics! Use them sparingly for greater effect. The rhyme 'thirty days hath September ...' helps us to remember the number of days in each month of the year. A well-known mnemonic for remembering the chemical constituents of coal is NO CASH, where N stands for Nitrogen, O for Oxygen, C for Carbon, A for Ash, S for Sulphur and H for Hydrogen.

If you have difficulty finding the letter combinations to make up words, use an aid such as *The Word Game Winning Dictionary* by Bruce Wetterau, a Signet Book, or other 'Scrabble' aid word books. A good dictionary and *Roget's Thesaurus* are indispensable. Use mnemonics and visual imagination to put fun back into learning, making it personalized, exciting and enjoyable, as it should be.

Examples of business mnemonics

A mnemonist is a person with a trained memory. Why not use some of the devices these experts use? Examples of mnemonics are:

- PEST – Political, Economic, Social and Technological – for environment analysis.

- PAIN – Payback, Accounting rate of return, Internal rate of return and Net present value – for investment appraisal methods.

- ARSES – Ad hoc, Representative, Standing, Executive and Subcommittees – for types of management committees.

- PLOCS – Planning, Leading, Organizing, Controlling and Staffing – for the main functions of management.

- SREDIM – Select, Record, Examine, Develop, Install and Maintain – the work study approach to solving problems. It can also be adapted and used to recall the key steps in the problem-solving or decision-making process.

- AIDA – Attention, Interest, Desire and Action – an aspect of sales promotion.

- DAGMAR – Defining Advertising Goals for Measured Advertising Results.

- SPEWSIC – Strategic objectives, Position audit, Environmental analysis, WOTS up analysis, Strategies to fill the gap, Implementation and Control – for the strategic planning process.

- SMART – Specific, Measurable, Attainable, Realistic and Timely – the characteristics of good objectives.

- APES – Annual plan, Profitability, Efficiency and Strategic – the major controls in a business.

To remember the names of the planets in our solar system use the sentence 'My Very Educated Mother Just Showed Us Nine Planets' – Mercury, Venus, Earth, Mars, Jupiter, Saturn, Uranus, Neptune and Pluto. The colours of the rainbow can easily be remembered by 'Richard Of York Gave Battle In Vain' – Red, Orange, Yellow, Green, Blue, Indigo and Violet.

You probably know the memory device for remembering that stalaCtites hang from the Ceiling of Caves, while stalaGmites grow from the Ground. Principle and principal are two words which are often misspelt and confused. To remember them for all time learn 'Principle is a rule while principal is a pal'.

If you have problems remembering how to spell 'believe' just remember 'Never believe a lie'. To distinguish 'stationery' from 'stationary', visualize a large Envelope for stationery. Why not invent your own mnemonics for important areas of your studies or work, or for vital information that you need to remember? Research shows that people who use mnemonics when they are studying a list learn two or three times better than those who use other methods.

Memory and drugs

Alertness and concentration are vital to successful reading and studying. Alcohol and drugs, apart from destroying brain cells and ruining your health, impede concentration and should not be taken when reading or studying. The occasional cup of tea or coffee will help you stay alert. Try to keep physically fit and eat a nutritious diet – maintaining health is an important aspect of studying for professional exams.

Video/Audio cassettes and computer-based training

Open University programmes on BBC and television business programmes generally will cover various subjects of interest to you. The Open University has many excellent lectures on economics, management, accountancy, finance, information technology and so on. Use your video recorder for review purposes. You might be able to persuade your training officer to hire or purchase some of the better lectures from the BBC or elsewhere for viewing. There is now a wide variety of management topics available on video and cassette tapes. You can listen to audiotapes while commuting to and from work, thereby utilizing time which otherwise would be wasted. Study subjects which are relevant to your career. Does your company have an open learning centre? Use its services to keep up to date on management and related topics of interest to you.

Summary

The mnemonic OPTIMISTIC will help you recall most of the memory aids in this chapter:

- Ongoing recall for permanent memory storage
- Pose questions for active learning
- Techniques (PLAN – Place, Link, Alphabet, Number rhyme, shape, phonetic systems) for organized learning
- Interest to enhance recall
- Mnemonics
- Integrate into your life
- STM v LTM
- Thinking/Reflection
- Imagination and visualization
- Categorization and chunking.

Be optimistic about your ability to develop a good memory. Believe in yourself. If you think you can, you will. If you think you can't, you won't. Practise the memory techniques outlined in this chapter.

Chapter 5   Use this page to draw your own Mind Map® of this chapter

6 Note-taking and Mind Maps®

- How should I take notes?
- What note-taking techniques are available?
- What are Mind Maps®?
- How do I draw Mind Maps®?
- What are the advantages of Mind Maps®?

The value of notes

There are good reasons why you should take notes. First, they speed up the task of review. It is a waste of valuable revision time if you reread your reports or business books in full. If your notes are well made, with key points and essential definitions for memorization included, it is only necessary to review the notes.

Secondly, the taking of notes at meetings or during training sessions keeps you actively involved. The writing activity uses your visual and kinaesthetic (i.e. sensation and muscle) functions which aids concentration and reinforces the memory. It follows from the task of trying to ascertain key points and concepts for inclusion in your notes. Of course, the main advantage of notes is that they are a permanent record for review.

Thirdly, people who take and use notes are generally more effective at recalling information than people who don't. Review your notes periodically, especially for critical information! For good organization and flexibility store them in a loose-leaf binder. They can thus be classified and added to as your knowledge increases.

Fourthly, note-taking is a good test of your listening, comprehension and short-term memory retention skills. Notes can also form the basis for discussion and research with your work colleagues.

Note-taking techniques

There are three basic note-taking techniques:

1   Outline notes.
2   Detailed notes.
3   Mind Maps®.

Outline notes are compiled by listing trigger words which conjure up mental images of the key concepts and ideas in the main text. Outline notes are generally kept in conventional linear format. They may be transferred to pocket-sized cards which can be carried about and revised as the opportunity presents itself, for example, while commuting in a bus or train. This might be a good way of preparing for that vital presentation to senior management.

Detailed notes are the format used by many people. You may be tempted to take down verbatim the content of a business or training presentation, afraid that you might miss something important. If the presentation has been logically presented the notes may stand without further revision. However, this may not be the case, and the notes may require editing and reorganization. Often they need additions involving further reading, research and reflection.

Because of its similarity to a spider's web the pattern form of note-taking is sometimes called a spider's web diagram. They are also known as Mind Maps® which are a method of notetaking offering great flexibility and which overcome the disadvantages of outline and detailed notetaking. Mind Maps® are explored in detail later in this chapter.

Writing notes

When reading a business book or pre-course notes supplied by your training department don't start reading at page one and continue until the end. Use the SQ3R method – SURVEY, QUESTION, READ, RECALL and REVIEW. This method will be dealt with in detail in the next chapter. It is sufficient to say here that notes should not be taken until the RECALL step. Write up your notes and review as soon as possible after a training session or meeting. Also, read up background material beforehand to make the session and the note-taking more meaningful.

Most business books and textbooks are divided into chapters, sections, subsections and paragraphs. For note-taking purposes, it is important to highlight the main ideas and definitions to help you remember them. This is not as difficult a task as it seems.

The overall concept in a chapter of a business book is contained in the chapter title. The main ideas of the chapter are shown in the title of the sections. Supporting points are in the title of the subsections. Important details are somewhere in the paragraphs. This is the part where you must use your head. Here are some tips.

The main idea of each paragraph should be in the first sentence or summarized in the last sentence. The first sentence is the topic sentence which introduces the main point, while the last sentence either quickly summarizes the content of the paragraph or introduces the point in the next paragraph. By concentrating on the first and last sentence of a paragraph you should understand the main theme of the paragraph. Watch out for VERBAL (words in italics or bold type) and VISUAL SIGNPOSTS (diagrams, pictures and charts) which will help you pick out and understand important points.

Use your own words when compiling your notes. Progressive educationalists now recommend an outline form of note-taking called Mind Maps®. These may be used, depending on individual taste, in preference to the more conventional methods of linear note-taking. Examples of Mind Maps® are given at the end of this book (see p. 155).

Mind Maps® and the brain

A Mind Map® is a non-linear, spatial, graphical technique where the subject matter is crystallized in a central image. The main themes of the subject radiate from the central image as branches. Branches comprise a key image or key word printed on an associated line. Topics of lesser importance are also represented as branches attached to higher level branches. The branches form a connected nodal structure. Mind Maps® may be enhanced and enriched with colour, pictures, codes, symbols and dimension to add interest. These enhancements aid memory, comprehension, motivation and the recall of information.

For example, in note-taking a Mind Map® may be a visual presentation and outline of the key words of a chapter, say, in a business book or self-development programme. You can draw a series of micro Mind Maps® for each chapter of a business book and a macro Mind Map® for the entire text. You will then have an outline macro Mind Map® of the entire book, supported by outline micro Mind Maps® of each chapter.

Mind Maps® are only one method of diagrammatic representation of information that have been used in business and education for more than twenty years. With the advent of computer graphics, including mind mapping software programmes, the use of such methods is becoming more popular and accessible. Other diagrammatic representational systems include tables, graphs, barcharts, flowcharts, organization charts, decisions trees, Venn diagrams, algorithms and so on. All these devices incorporate abbreviated verbal information, within non-linear spatial layouts, often with colour. They differ from Mind Maps® in that they have a specific, rather than a general, use. For example, flowcharts as used by work study practitioners or systems analysts are a diagrammatic representation of a business procedure. By such methods complex systems can be grasped quickly, analysed and made more efficient. Tables and graphs are very useful for displaying statistical information. Mind Maps®, on the other hand, are general purpose models that retain the advantages of verbal and graphical representation by using words, images, symbols and colour while maintaining a great deal of flexibility.

Making Mind Maps®

Most people are unfamiliar with mind mapping. The process will therefore be discussed in some detail and related to the underlying theories. The following rules are based on the Buzan method:

1   *Use an A4 sheet (or A3 if necessary) of blank paper.* Draw the Mind Map® in landscape rather than portrait style. This gives you more space to work with. The advantage of using standard 'A' sizes is obvious from the point of view of availability, photocopying, filing and so on.

2   *Start the Mind Map® in the centre of the page and radiate out.* This is in contrast to linear notes that start at the top lefthand side of the page and work down. Draw a multicoloured image in the centre to indicate the core and theme of the Mind Map®. Start in the centre because this reflects the connective way that the brain thinks. This allows more space and freedom for developing ideas. Use image and colour because the old Confucian saying 'a picture speaks more than a thousand words' applies to both memory and creativity.

    Psychologists have shown that images linked to words aid recall. Sketching is a most important aspect of the process because in figuring out how to draw a concept, the maker increases his understanding of it. Moving from verbalization of an idea to visual representation requires thinking about that idea in a new way. It means considering elements that may not have suggested themselves before, and discovering new possibilities. Therefore, making images on Mind Maps® encodes the information more strongly in memory and aids recall and comprehension.

3   *Attach main themes to the central image.* The brain works by association. Print words in large capital letters on top of thick

lines having the same length as the words. The large capital letters and thick lines emphasize the hierarchy and significance of ideas by making them more visible and thus more memorable. The linked nature of the Mind Map® reflects the associative and connective nature of the brain. Some psychologists maintain that human memory is a vast, intricately interconnected network. According to such models it is not letters, syllables, or words that are recorded, but concepts and propositions. The propositions are then related in various ways to other propositions, forming an associative network. The act of encoding an event is simply forming new links and associations in the network. Mind Maps® show the links and relationships between key concepts giving users an overview and a greater insight and understanding of the topic.

4   *Use a hayfork or fishbone technique to connect subsidiary lines to main lines.* These reflect the logic and associative nature of the brain. Psychologists have long established that people learn by associating new knowledge to existing knowledge and experience.

5   *Print single key words on the connecting lines.* Preferably one word per line. Each key word has it own range of many possible connections. Placing the key word alone on a line gives the brain more freedom to branch out in a connective fashion from that word. Phrases hide the individual word, and reduce the possibilities of further links and associations, creativity and clarity of memory. These radiant lines give the Mind Map® its basic connective and associative structure. Traditional linear notes give little opportunity to add our own organization and association. Printing on Mind Maps® takes longer but it is worth the effort as it gives impact and photographic feedback to the user. Two-dimensional lettering can be used to make specific key words stand out. This is in line with the Von Restorff effect in psychology, which suggests that things are remembered better if they are made unusual. Making words unique and outstanding is an important feature of Mind Maps®.

6 *Use colour throughout.* Colour further enhances the Mind Map® making it more interesting, unique and outstanding and improving retention and recall. Fun and relaxation facilitates learning. This is one of the underlying assumptions of accelerated learning. It is easier to learn new things when you are relaxed and enjoying yourself. When you are bored learning takes longer, you will tire faster, you will forget quicker and you will need to revise more often. Colour stimulates thought, creativity and memory and appeals to the aesthetic senses. It will increase the brain's pleasure in building the Mind Map®. Colour also increases interest and provides motivation to return to it for review. Psychologists maintain that colour is an important tool in visual thinking. It separates ideas, stimulates creativity, and aids memory. Colour captures and directs attention. Even linear notes can benefit from colour coding: maps, cluster maps, mandalas, and most expressive drawings are more effective in colour. Highlighting a key idea or point in yellow will make you, or your audience, perceive the point first. Yellow highlighters are ideal for emphasizing key points on the Mind Map®.

7 *Use images, drawings, symbols and codes.* Personalize the contents to represent main themes. Tests have shown that a sharp, interactive image can improve recall of word pairs by 300 per cent compared with single rote learning. Images improve problem solving and communication and over time will improve a person's perceptual skills. Images together with colour make the content of the Mind Maps® more memorable. Geniuses including Einstein and da Vinci used images in their work. For example, Einstein's ideas came to him initially as pictures and images which he subsequently translated into words and mathematical symbols. It is widely reported that he arrived at his theory of relativity while dreaming. He visualized what it would be like to travel down a sunbeam. Similarly Kekule, a German chemist, discovered the molecular structure of benzene while dozing in front of the fire allowing the pattern of flames to inspire him. Da Vinci is famous for his scientific and artistic

talents. Extrapolating from this, the inclusion of images on Mind Maps® should help retention, recall and the generation of ideas. It is noticeable in the great scientific advances throughout history that people combined imagination and intuition with careful reasoned analysis. It was the partnership of right and left brain that made the crucial difference. Mind Maps® harmonize left- and right-brain thinking and enhance creativity and crystallize ideas. Unless ideas are recorded they are forgotten. Ideas externalized in a Mind Map® can be explored, extended, enhanced and experimented with.

8   *Segment the main themes by drawing boundary lines around them.* This gives the Mind Map® its unique brain patterned shape. Miller's magical number 7 plus or minus 2 rule in psychology suggests that major segments should not number more than 9. Mind Maps® chunk information into meaningful groups by a process of segmentation. In most practical situations there are seldom more than seven or eight subcentres, so the material in a Mind Map® can be organized into a number of easily remembered chunks. Similarly, the number of chunks radiating from each subcentre again will usually be within the immediate memory capacity. Mind Maps® can thus capitalize on the chunking principle by careful organization and grouping of words within segments to maximize learning and recall.

9   *Use personalized codes and well-known abbreviations.* For example, 'Mgt' for management and 'Ctee' for committee etc. This saves space and speeds up processing, encoding and registration of information. Personalized codes using colours and arrows add a fourth dimension to Mind Maps®. They enhance the mind mapper's ability to analyse, define, structure, organize and reason. Studies in psychology show that it is far easier for people to remember information if it is personalized.

10   *To make information more memorable invent mnemonics for key points.* Use these as memory aids. Mnemonics have a long track record. They go back to Greek and Roman times when their usefulness

for remembering key points was first recognized. Thomas Aquinas used mnemonic systems for teaching his monks. They were used by some of the kings of England and France, and by Shakespeare, Francis Bacon and Leibnitz. Children at school use them without any prompting, and they are the secret formula behind mnemonists. Although still not considered totally respectable by some academics, psychologists have established that they can indeed improve recall. Some mnemonists recall information by forming idiosyncratic verbal associations for the material they want to memorize. Visual imagery mnemonics are an extremely effective way of remembering lists of words, and words that are converted into images are more easily memorized than those that are not. The method of loci is one of the oldest mnemonic devices. Mind Maps® are a method of loci and an important mnemonic device. The segments are general locations, while the branches are more specific locations. The locations can be used to associate a series of items to be learnt. Memory and mnemonics are explored further in Chapter 5.

How to identify key words

Keyword notes are far easier to recall than phrases or sentences. The brain operates on the basis of key words and images rather than sentences. It automatically drops the inessentials, and we should do the same in note-taking. The advantages of key words are:

- The quantity of words is significantly reduced, facilitating faster review and revision.
- The recorded words, if chosen appropriately, are rich in imagery.
- The very act of extracting the key words improves concentration, understanding and the depth of processing.

Identifying the key words are an important aspect of the mind mapping process. The following are a few pointers which will help you to pick out the key points from a text when drawing up Mind Map® outline notes:

1 *Hierarchy of ideas.* When producing the Mind Map® from texts use the hierarchy of ideas concept for choosing key words. In the case of the chapter the title should give you the main idea. Note the section titles for the main ideas of the sections. The subsections should give you the important supporting points. In other words, follow the author's organizational structure. Psychologists have found that subjects who are shown words in hierarchies, do far better in recall experiments than those who are shown random lists. So structure and organization in Mind Maps® aids recall. In business books and textbooks questions at the end of each chapter should alert you as to what the author considers to be the key issues in the chapter and thus the key issues for your Mind Maps®.

2 *Paragraphs.* It is well established that the first sentence of a paragraph is usually the topic sentence containing the main idea of the paragraph. The key word or words in the topic sentence may sometimes be in italics. If so, the author has identified the main idea for you. Also remember that the last sentence of the paragraph may summarize the key point or introduce the key point in the next paragraph. The first paragraph of a chapter may give you a quick preview while the last paragraph may summarize what has gone before or what comes next. Similarly, the first or last chapter may give an overview of the book. Of course, a summary at the end of a chapter, if provided, is the author's way of outlining the chapter's main ideas. Study this carefully for valuable cues as to the key points for your Mind Map®.

3 *Visual signposts.* Visual signposts in a text emphasize important points. They can be in the following formats: words in italics; words underlined; words in bold face; numbering of points; and lettering of points. Other visual signposts may be in the form of tables, graphs, pictures, diagrams, algorithms, models and charts. Some people skip over these, rather than examining them closely which is worthwhile. These 'models' will clarify difficult concepts

and aid comprehension and may be usefully incorporated in your Mind Map®. Remember, the more images on the Mind Map®, the better the recall; diagrams, which use the right hemisphere, and words, which use the left, employ both sides of the brain.

4 *Verbal signposts*. Authors use verbal signposts to introduce important points. For example, 'firstly, secondly …' means about to list details. 'On the other hand' means about to contradict a point. 'However' means about to make known a qualification. 'For instance' means about to introduce examples. 'Therefore' means about to draw conclusions. These are useful cues to help you pick out the key words for your Mind Map®.

5 *The Pareto Principle*. The 80:20 rule in marketing signifies that a small proportion (20 per cent) of customers may account for a large proportion (80 per cent) of the value of the business's turnover. Applied to writing it suggests that a large proportion of words are superfluous and redundant – structure words, such as 'and', 'the', 'to', etc. – and are not needed for an understanding of key concepts. The reader's job is to identify key words. This is one of the principles on which Mind Maps® are based. Sometimes people cannot understand because they fail to see the wood for the trees. Avoid this by concentrating on key words and images. Mind Maps® thus save considerable time when used as part of a review plan.

6 *Recall words*. Psychologists have long established that effective learners learn concepts and broad principles rather than cluttering their minds with detail. Thus, key words should be those that bring to mind the key concepts of the text. The more concrete they are the more memorable. Concrete words converted to visual images are on the whole more easily remembered than abstract words, for which imagery is difficult. Nouns and adjectives are the easiest words to remember because they can be visualized. Thus recall words are usually nouns. They are words that trigger off other words and images. They are the hooks on which other words can be linked.

Uses of Mind Maps®

You can of course use the Mind Map® technique for applications other than note-taking, for example:

1   *Taking lectures.* Use a spaced listening technique. Listen for 2 to 3 minutes, then write for half a minute. Repeat the process. Use key words only and structure the Mind Map® as you go along. After the lecture restructure the Mind Map® if necessary. This technique gives the listener more time to concentrate and reflect on the key issues of the lecture rather than being overwhelmed by superfluous detail. Other than by shorthand it is physically impossible to take down a lecture word for word as it is spoken. It is estimated by psychologists that speakers talk at the rate of about 135 words per minute while we can only write at about 40wpm. Therefore, trying to take notes verbatim may result in us missing most of the lecture. Mind Maps are a type of shorthand and will also help you focus on essential issues.

2   *Giving lectures and public speaking.* Why not use the Mind Map® technique to prepare your talk? This will drastically cut down your preparation time and give a natural flow to the delivery. Mind Maps® facilitate the lecturer in maintaining eye contact with the audience – a most important aspect of effective presentations. It also provides the flexibility to stay within time. One Mind Map® sheet will substitute for many cue cards or sheets that can fall and get out of sequence at the worst possible moment causing much embarrassment and distress. Mind Maps® are imprinted on the mind during their preparation because of the concentration required to prepare them and their unique format so that recall and review is facilitated. Psychologist and author, Michael J. Gelb, has written a book called *Present Yourself* on the topic of public speaking based entirely on the Mind Map® approach. In fact, he uses a series of Mind Maps® to summarize the content of the chapters in his book. Mind Maps® may also be distributed to students as advance organizers. Initially students may be confused

by the unconventional layout, but after a familiarization process their response to Mind Maps® is almost universally favourable. Students use them as skeletal overviews to add to and customize, if they wish, while listening to the lecture. They also use them for revision and review purposes. The more personalized the students make Mind Maps® the more effective they are as learning instruments.

3   *Writing and reports.* Use the Mind Map® technique for creating ideas and planning your report. This will improve the clarity, conciseness, coherence, organization, logic and sequencing of the content of your report. In a business context Mind Maps® can banish writer's block from letters, reports and memos. For report writing use the Mind Map® technique for planning and creating ideas. Key points can be used as headings while the supporting points can be used as subheadings. In reading complex reports use Mind Maps® for review purposes and for a quick overview of the key issues. They encourage creativity by gradually building up an outline as the ideas emerge. Similarly they can be used to plan books, articles, essays, assignments and dissertations. Mind Maps® are a useful way of condensing, integrating, digesting and overviewing information from many sources, including research, experience, observation and reflection. They help structure assignments in a systematic, holistic and logical fashion. Much time can be saved by using this approach.

4   *Minutes.* What better way to quickly summarize the proceedings of a meeting than by the use of key words in a Mind Map®! On a single page you can represent all the dynamics of a meeting and grasp its essence without reviewing pages of notes. The Mind Map® can then be used to draw up the formal minutes. It can be used to streamline meetings. It improves note-taking, increases idea generating, facilitates group problem solving and simplifies communication. It increases productivity and saves time.

5   *Creativity and brainstorming.* Why not use the Mind Map® technique for creativity, problem solving and analysis? It can be used

individually or for teamwork. In business Mind Maps® have been used in areas such as marketing, manufacturing, research and development, finance, strategic planning and training and development.

6   *Study*. Students find Mind Maps® very useful as a study technique in the areas of note-taking, recall and revision. They are also a very good planning aid for essays, assignments and dissertations. In the exam room they can be used as a planning aid when answering questions.

Mind Map® advantages

The linear method of note-taking presents many problems including deciding in what order to list facts. Where will you start? When will you end? You will have problems inserting additions and making deletions as necessary. However, the biggest disadvantage of conventional presentation is that it presents a homogeneous field which is difficult to learn and become motivated about and organize in a meaningful way. A Mind Map® is a FRAMEWORK, organizing ideas and their advantages. The mnemonic FRAMEWORK stands for:

Flexible. Mind Maps® can be developed with new and additional pieces of information by extending the appropriate branch. With linear notes this creates organizational problems. Adding to Mind Maps® may result from serious and pastime reading, watching television, listening to radio, observation, discussion, experience and critical and reflective thought. These additions may be cross-referenced to their original sources. The resultant Mind Map® is a comprehensive, concentrated, conceptualized, integrated, visual and easily digestible overview and key word summary of a topic. Psychologists have found that the major circuitry of the brain is laid down by birth, but the details and fine tuning continue to develop throughout life. Indeed, experience itself can cause new synapses to grow. Knowledge and experiences, then, can shape the brain. Let the Mind Map® be a physical manifestation of your increased knowledge and brainpower!

Recall, review and revise. Rereading of textbooks, study manuals and distance learning modules is kept to a minimum. Mind Maps® save time, and in preparing for professional examinations and university degrees, especially on a part-time basis while holding down a full-time job often with family commitments, time management is critical to success. Recall and review are essential to consolidate information in long-term memory and to optimize study effectiveness. A Mind Map® with its key words, particularly if these are converted into mnemonics, is much easier to learn than twenty pages of linear notes. Also, the various mnemonics should be linked to each other or associated with existing stores of knowledge. Systematic review of Mind Maps® will imprint the contents into your long-term memory.

Associations. Knowledge is in fact a pattern of connected ideas. It is the association of new information to existing stores of knowledge and experience that makes new knowledge meaningful. Therefore, Mind Maps® will help to improve your memory. Meaningful learning happens when a person explicitly ties new knowledge previously learnt to relevant concepts or propositions. Relationships among concepts are more accessible in a two-dimensional display than in text. Knowing how ideas are related is important for memorization. The node-link relationship in Mind Maps® helps the learner to assimilate new facts and perceive how detailed information links to the central concept. Therefore, Mind Maps® by their unique brain-patterned spatial structure will help you to recall trigger words and their many associations, while linking the words to each other and to the central concept.

Multidimensional brain. Psychological research has shown that the brain is a multidimensional and multiordinate phenomenon. Mind Maps® are analogous to the brain's own system of making connections and interconnections. They integrate analytical and holistic thinking: analytical in the form of words, sequence and organization; holistic in the form of images, associations, creativity, integration and overview. Mind Maps®, through an interconnective model of words and images, help people integrate both sides of their brain and contribute to whole brain learning.

Essence. The overall concept or essence, highlighted at the centre of the Mind Map®, with the hierarchy of ideas leading from it, provides a very clear overview. Some executives fail to grasp the essentials of reports or business books, not because of insufficient work and preparation but because they clutter up their minds with detail and are thus unable to see the wood for the trees – a type of 'paralysis by analysis'. Effective learning means working smarter rather than harder. It means learning concepts and broad principles rather than cluttering up the mind with details. Summarizing the key points in a presentation is critical to effective learning. This final step helps executives see the big picture. It helps them overview, integrate and relate the key aspects of the report or presentation and see clearly the critical issues.

In memorizing anything an overview is vital so that you understand the broad principles involved before you begin. A Mind Map® is an overview of the key points of a text and thus aids memorization and comprehension. When information is simply listed, it is difficult to prioritize ideas. It is also hard to see relationships, connect ideas, and see the 'big picture', and the result is a lot of information with no form or hierarchy of significance. The Mind Map® structure graphically connects all ideas and shows the significance of each in relation to each other and to the centre.

Worthwhile visual aid. A picture is worth more than a thousand words. A Mind Map® is in fact a visual aid with impact, originality and creativity. The effectiveness of our learning is increased the more we bring our senses into play, particularly the visual senses. Psychologists tell us that impressions come 84 per cent through the eyes, 9 per cent through the ears and 7 per cent through the other senses. Hence the importance of visual images and Images linked to words improve recall even more effectively. Why not practise mentally walking the Mind Map®? With training and practice, most people can improve their capacity to use images. Visualizing Mind Maps® in your mind's eye will provide the training and practice and thus increase your skill at creating mental images.

Organized. Mind Maps® are a structured and systematic way of organizing information and facts. Just as road maps differentiate between major roads, minor roads and byways, so can key concepts, important ideas and important detail be differentiated by the thickness of lines, codes, dimensions, colours and so on. Organization is one of the key components of a good memory. Structure influences how incoming text information is organized. Text content for which readers have a structure is said to be better organized, elaborated and remembered. For instance, researchers have shown that a narrative about a fictitious soccer game is better recalled by readers who are knowledgeable about soccer than those who are not. Background knowledge helps learning of new material, and advance organizers and structure provide the key concepts that facilitate learning and retention. Context provides a way of organizing information beforehand, therefore making it more memorable. Mind Maps® provide the structure, organization and context to learn. They link new information to existing stores of knowledge in a structured framework facilitating comprehension, learning and memory.

Reconnaissance. Mind Maps® will help you carry out a reconnaissance. In the Wild West this was the function of the Indian scout. A Mind Map®, therefore, maps out unfamiliar terrain particularly when used to preview chapters and whole books. Similarly, good drivers plan unfamiliar routes by advance study of road maps. The mapping activity which Mind Maps® entail imprints the information on the student's brain, making it part of his own experience and knowledge. Previewing outlines improves learning and recall by establishing a framework and creating hooks for associating new information.

Knowledge of lefthand and righthand brain. The brain is divided into two separate halves. The left side, or scientific brain, deals with language, numbers, logic and analysis. The right side, or creative brain, deals with images, rhythm, colour and daydreaming. Mind Maps® are an effective means of integrating both hemispheres. There is increasing evidence that the ability to put thoughts into images as well as words enhances thinking skills and improves intelligence. So the benefits of Mind Maps® extend far beyond the practical application of recording ideas to higher order thinking and increased intelligence.

Mind mapping and conventional note-taking

Mind Maps® start in the centre and radiate out. Conventional note-taking starts at the top lefthand side of the page and works down from left to right in a listlike manner.

Mind Maps® use key words and images – and save time. Conventional note-taking uses phrases and abbreviated sentences. Key words may be obscured in the clutter of verbiage and time is wasted. The open-ended nature of Mind Maps® makes them easy to add to. Inserting and adding points can be cumbersome with linear notes.

The Mind Map® structure uses lines in a tree of evolution fashion on which the key and supporting words are placed. The relationship of key concepts and ideas is apparent and a quick overview is realized. Recall is facilitated. The links between each line in conventional note-taking are not easily seen. As you move on to the next page any links between the pages are lost. Items are difficult to remember.

The Mind Map® technique uses colour, images, capital letters, codes, lines and connecting lines, and segmentation to emphasize, group and distinguish ideas, which are not a feature of conventional note-taking. The colour and images in Mind Maps® make them fun and relaxing to do and create interest and motivation. Linear notes create monotony and boredom and negative associations of bygone punitive school days. Mind Maps® facilitate the parallel processing of words in the same way the brain is thought to function. Linear note-taking encourages sequential processing of words which is contrary to the way that the brain is now thought to work.

Mind Maps® induce relaxation and help to integrate the creative insights and imagery associated with the right brain and the words and logic associated with the left brain, giving you whole-brain learning. Linear notes may prove stressful and stifle creativity. The Mind Map® gives a birdseye view of a topic which is readily available. An overview of a topic is not as quickly seen from linear notes. Concepts are lost in homogeneous pages of unrelieved linear script.

There is increasing evidence in literature that Mind Maps® are more effective than conventional note-taking in aiding comprehension and recall. Because of their tree of evolution, hierarchy of significance, open-ended structure with the emphasis on links and associations they facilitate brainstorming, creativity and problem solving. Linear notes, on the other hand, inhibit creativity because of the sequential structure that may create writer's block. Linear notes also limit our ability to see the big picture and make new insights and connections. The 'big picture' is obvious from a Mind Map®.

Summary

- The main argument for note-taking is that executives are able to review and recall critical information quickly and efficiently. Notes should be categorized and filed neatly for reference in a loose-leaf binder.

- The SQ3R method facilitates good note-taking. It is best to make notes at the recall step. Mind Maps® are recommended in preference to the more conventional method of linear note-taking. The rules of mind mapping are:
  – use an A4 sheet of blank paper
  – start in the centre of the page and radiate out
  – attach main themes to the central image
  – use a hayfork or fishbone technique to connect subsidiary lines to main lines
  – print single key words on the connecting lines
  – use colour throughout
  – ideally use images, drawings, symbols and codes throughout

– segment the main themes by drawing boundary lines around each theme
– use personalized codes and well-known abbreviations
– invent mnemonics for key points for better recall.

- In addition to study, Mind Maps® can be used for a wide variety of purposes including making presentations, public speaking, minute taking, report writing, creativity, brainstorming and problem solving.

- The advantages of Mind Maps® can be recalled by the mnemonic FRAMEWORK:
  – *Flexible*
  – *Recall*
  – *Associations*
  – *Multidimensional brain*
  – *Essence*
  – *Worthwhile visual aid*
  – *Organized*
  – *Reconnaissance*
  – *Knowledge of lefthand and righthand brain.*

Chapter 6   Use this page to draw your own Mind Map® of this chapter

7 Effective reading

- What are the barriers to effective reading?
- What is the SQ3R method?
- How are visual and verbal signposts used to emphasize important points?
- How can I improve my concentration?
- How can I improve my reading skills?
- What are the goal-focused approaches to reading?

Better reading

Before you can become a more effective reader you should recognize some of the barriers to meaningful reading. A lack of understanding of written matter may not be your fault. It may be because of the author's poor presentation. When buying business books or textbooks make sure they meet some of the following criteria. They should be well laid out with clear signposting, free from ambiguity, indexed, easy to read and understand, cover the subject effectively and in the case of technical books include a glossary. Most important of all, you should feel comfortable with your book. In practice you may have to look around for some time before you find a book that meets your particular needs.

SQ3R

For better reading use the SQ3R method: Survey, Question, Read, Recall and Review. This technique will help you to anticipate information and discriminate between what is important to your purpose, what is less important and what is irrelevant. It will prime your knowledge base and facilitate the integration and understanding of the text to follow. Prioritize your reading on a 'must know', 'should know' and 'nice to know' basis. The latter can be scanned through. The SQ3R method will make your reading active, purposeful and more concentrated. When you are reading, try and find the main idea. Pick out the important details and evaluate what you are reading. Let's now look at the SQ3R technique in more detail.

Survey

The survey stage, which takes five to ten minutes, is initially applied to the whole book. Later you will apply it to each chapter and section. This stage can be conveniently subdivided into three parts: overview, preview and inview. Survey is in fact a reconnaissance of the unfamiliar terrain in the book to enable you to build up reference points.

Overview

The first part of the survey stage is the overview, where you familiarize yourself with the plan of the book. Look at the title page and cover. This should give an idea of the general subject matter, the level of reader, the date of publication and the author's name, background and qualifications. Has it been written with a particular audience in mind?

The next stage is to study the preface (often called the foreword, introduction etc.). It will tell you why the author wrote the book and who was its target reader. The preface will also give you the scope and purpose of the book, its outline and structure and method of use.

Now turn to the table of contents for an overview of the topics dealt with. It will also familiarize you with the author's plan, organization and layout. After this study the index at the back of the book. Skim through the entries. Anything familiar or that you are already expert in? Look up the relevant section and see how the author has dealt with it. Compare this with what you know about the topic. By this technique you can judge the author's competence and knowledge of the subject and the suitability of the book for you.

Decide whether it is necessary to read the whole book or only parts relevant to your purpose. You'll have time enough to read the whole book if you're still interested, after solving your immediate objective.

Preview

Preview the contents. Skim through the book. Read the chapter and section headings. Study with particular care any charts, models, diagrams, tables, pictures and graphs. The author has included these because they will illustrate some important concepts where words alone would be inadequate. If preparing for exams, bear in mind that the ability to illustrate points by including diagrams, drawings, models or graphs wins valuable marks, for the same reason they are a substitute for word spinning. Glance at the occasional sentences.

Inview

Now apply the same approach that you used to the book as a whole, but this time to each chapter. Carry out a detailed survey of each chapter. Study the chapter heading, section headings, subsection headings and the first and last sentence of each paragraph. Write down the two or three key concepts covered in each paragraph. Notice the relative size of headings or classification system used for clues as to the importance of ideas, organization and structure.

Depending on your purpose, completion of any of these stages may meet your needs without going any further. For example, if you only need an overview of a topic these stages in themselves may be sufficient.

Question

There is a famous questioning technique familiar to Organization and Methods or Research people – What? Why? When? How? Where? Who? It puts you in a critical frame of mind. The following verse by Rudyard Kipling will help you remember this questioning technique:

> I keep six honest serving-men
> (They taught me all I knew);
> Their names are What and Why and When
> And How and Where and Who.

Set down the state of your own knowledge of the subject in the form of a Mind Map®. Add areas to be explored, representing gaps in your knowledge and questions to be answered.

Many business books and textbooks have questions at the end of each chapter. Before tackling the chapter it is a good idea to look at these questions. Study the chapter with a view to answering them. The questions are in fact the author's method of highlighting important points essential to the proper understanding of the subject.

Read

Always read with a purpose. Actively seek answers to questions you have already constructed and you are likely to learn. Look for the main idea of the book, chapter, section and paragraph. This is called the HIERARCHY OF IDEAS and is at four levels: level 1, the book itself; level 2, the chapters; level 3, the sections; and level 4, the paragraphs.

The survey stage is always concerned with levels 1, 2 and 3. The read stage is concerned with in-depth study at level 4.

At the first reading don't take notes. Also, don't underline. This destroys a book. The best plan is to mark the important sentences vertically along the margin lightly in pencil. If you come to a stumbling block skip over it after marking it with a question mark. It may not be essential to the understanding of the rest of the chapter. In any event the material further on may explain more adequately the problem causing the stumbling block. Then go back over it and you may find that you thoroughly understand it. The worst thing you could do when you come to a stumbling block is to become discouraged and give up. In any learning situation you will have periods of rapid progress, slow progress and no progress. This is known as the learning curve and periods of slow progress and no progress are called learning plateaus. There is nothing unique or unusual about your situation. It happens to all learners.

If you still don't understand the point causing the learning block, talk to your training officer, discuss it with your boss, with fellow learners or work colleagues. Read it again. Confirm in your own mind that you really have the main ideas at each of the levels. Pay attention to the important details at this stage. Mark on the margin lightly in pencil the important detail which you will eventually put on your Mind Map®.

Recall

Now you should begin to take notes by recalling what you have studied and making Mind Maps®. Complete your Mind Maps® by reference to the text. Remember the following advantages:

- Recall gives you an opportunity to discover any gaps in your knowledge which require remedial action. This is the learning principle of knowledge of results.
- Recall is an active rather than a passive method of study. By

summarizing your knowledge you are actively involved and getting to grips with the subject.

How often should you recall? Mentally recall the main ideas at the end of each section. Recall at the end of each paragraph would disrupt the flow and continuity in reading. How much time should you spend in recalling? Approximately half your time should be spent in recalling what you have read.

Make your notes. In fact we could call the SQ3R the SQ4R method, the fourth R standing for write. Use a Mind Map® to record the main ideas recalled. Complete the Mind Map® from the text. Reserve a column for definitions, rules, formulae, etc. Recitation is the best form of memorization. Remember that recall, recitation and paraphrasing mentally and in writing is a great way of imprinting information on your memory. In many work situations you will be required to recall large areas of knowledge without reference to notes or manuals. You are in fact judged to a significant extent in your business life by the amount you can recall.

Review

Unless you review immediately you forget 50 per cent of what you read and 80 per cent within twenty-four hours. Within a week 90 per cent will be forgotten and eventually almost everything. Maintain and improve your powers of concentration by adhering to a systematic review plan. Frequent review ensures that the material in your short-term memory (STM) is transferred to your long-term memory (LTM). Begin Mind Maps® at the recall stage and complete them at the review stage. Four or five readings of textbooks are normally required before their contents are in any way familiar. If you use the Mind Maps® for review these re-readings are not required. However, you should cross-reference them to the text. This will enable you to look up relevant points in the book when you wish to do so.

Review from the Mind Maps® immediately after reading, within 24 hours, after one week and again after one month. Review again after three months. The theory behind this is that after the third or fourth review, the information goes into your LTM. Once this happens you need not review as frequently. Another advantage of review is that the ideas fit together more coherently and there is thus less danger of having an erroneous concept in LTM. Of course, this review system is only worthwhile for critical information.

Main ideas

The main ideas of a book, or the hierarchy of ideas, is contained at four levels: level 1, the book title; level 2, the chapter titles; level 3, the section headings; and level 4, the paragraph. The topic sentence in each paragraph is usually the first sentence. The last sentence will be either a summary or lead into the main idea in the next paragraph. So look at the first and last sentence of each paragraph.

Read the chapter a second time for important details which will clarify, develop, support or illustrate the main ideas at the various levels. Look for VISUAL SIGNPOSTS. The author uses these to emphasize important points. Visual signposts can be in the following formats: (1) words in italics; (2) words underlined; (3) words in bold or different type face; (4) numbering of points; and (5) lettering of points.

Other visual signposts can be in the form of tables, graphs, pictures, diagrams and charts. A picture speaks more than a thousand words. Illustrations should be studied with this maxim in mind, because difficult and important concepts are often presented in an illustrative style for better understanding. Learn to draw these yourself to develop your right-brain skills.

The author may also employ VERBAL SIGNPOSTS to introduce important points as follows:

Verbal signposts:	*Means author is about to:*
1 First, second etc.	List details
2 On the other hand	Contradict a point
3 However	Introduce a qualification
4 For instance	Give examples

5 Furthermore	Support the main idea
6 Therefore	Draw conclusions
7 Again	Emphasize
8 So	Conclude or reinforce

Apply the questioning approach

When reading, adopt a 'doubting Thomas' approach. Evaluate the text in a critical and questioning way. Keep the following questions in the forefront of your mind:

1 Are the author's facts correct? In most reputable textbooks they probably are.
2 Does the author distinguish between facts, assumptions and opinions?
3 Are conclusions developed logically from the facts?
4 What other conclusions could be drawn?
5 Do you agree with the conclusions reached?
6 Are there contrary viewpoints?
7 Are some of the claims made unproved, or can they be supported by empirical research?

This questioning technique will make your reading more active and purposeful with a greater understanding and retention of the material. Watch out for limitations, exceptions, contradictions, arguments against any statement made, similarities and differences between theories discussed.

Relate the text to your own experience and more generally to your working environment. If you are learning about a topic outside your own area of expertise, talk to colleagues in your own or other departments and outside the company who may be able to help you put the ideas in context.

Faster reading

It has now been established that with training you can read considerably faster without any loss of comprehension. The average reader reads at a speed of 240 words per minute. This can be improved, with a little training, to 360 wpm. With sustained effort and plenty of practice you can achieve 600 wpm when reading easy material. President Kennedy is reputed to have had a reading speed of 1000 wpm. The average resting heart rate is 60 beats per second. Most books have about 10 to 12 words per line. A reading speed of one line per second results in both a rhythm of 60 beats a minute with the hand and allows the eye to read between 600 and 700 wpm. Make this speed your objective for most material. For more difficult material or for where you lack a conceptual background, and in order to maintain satisfactory comprehension levels, you should be satisfied with a reading rate of 400 wpm. Most experts consider a comprehension rate of 75 per cent or above to be adequate. On the other hand, according to research studies, there appears to be a minimal reading speed of 200 wpm below which the reader may fail to process the meaning of text effectively. Reading below 200 wpm apparently reflects inefficient, word-by-word reading which is not conducive to integrating and comprehending text in a meaningful way.

Research has also shown that when the term reading is interpreted in the sense of comprehending most of the words on a page, it is impossible to read faster than 800 to 1000 wpm and that comprehension suffers above a speed of 400 wpm. The capacity of the working memory is also a constraint. Of course, higher speeds can be achieved when methods such as skimming, scanning and skipping are employed, but this should be distinguished from genuine reading.

Recognition span

The eyes move with a jerky, intermittent motion. The brain reads words at each fixation. This means you can read only when your eyes momentarily stop, each stop is called a fixation. To be a faster reader, therefore, you must increase your RECOGNITION SPAN. The recognition or perceptual span is about three words. Reading for ideas by chunking words means that you will have fewer fixations, taking in larger groups of words with a faster reading speed.

Defects of poor readers

Poor readers generally suffer from the following defects:

- They have small recognition spans. They read each word individually. This makes the flow of their reading disjointed and hinders comprehension. Try to read a whole phrase instantaneously.

- They regress. Their eyes drift back to reread words and phrases. It shows a lack of confidence in their reading ability, as it is more than likely that they have absorbed what they have read. This habit destroys concentration. Regressing may also be caused by your eyes losing their place on the page.

- They vocalize. This is a hangover from schooldays and as a result speed and quality of reading suffer. In certain circumstances, such as revision, vocalizing can aid memory. Most readers subvocalize, i.e. say words internally to themselves. You can speed up your reading by not subvocalizing structure words, such as 'and', 'the' etc. However, subvocalizing key work's has been proved by psychologists to aid memory.

- Because poor readers have small recognition spans, they make many eye fixations which in turn slows down reading. Each fixation is also of longer duration than that used by good readers.

- Poor readers do not vary their reading speed in line with their purpose, level of knowledge and the difficulty of the reading matter. Good readers see more in less time and vary their reading rate in line with their purpose and the difficulty of the text.

- Poor readers fail to integrate prior knowledge and experience with text information and do not apply critical reading skills such as analysis, synthesis and evaluation to the written text.

- Poor readers may have a small working memory capacity and consequently less capacity for maintaining previous information and integrating new information. On the other hand, good readers with a large working memory should be able to retain more of a text in working memory while processing new text, so their integration of the information may be more thorough.

Reading techniques

Use to your benefit the different techniques of speed reading, skipping, skimming, scanning and reading slowly. Develop speed reading skills by applying the VERTIGO system (discussed in the next section). Skimming is where your eyes cover certain preselected sections of the text to gain a general overview. Scanning is when your eyes glance over material to find a particular piece of information. You could employ rapid or fast reading to advantage with a novel or a not too difficult text. Obviously with light material you can follow the story line without reading every word carefully. If you are reading for specific information, as in research, you should skip that matter which is not essential to your purpose. Use the index to advantage here.

To survey a book employ the skimming technique, by reading first and last chapters, first and last paragraphs in each chapter, signposts, first and last sentences of each paragraph and chapter summaries. Make one-word summaries of each paragraph and prepare Mind Maps® from these, if you need to grasp the book as a whole. Vary the depth of your survey in line with your purpose.

Finally, with difficult texts you must read slowly for comprehension. Slow reading is normally suitable for studying. But remember, vary your style of reading in line with the purpose. Read quickly material that you are already familiar with. Read slowly material that is new to you or that you find difficult.

Seven ways to improve your reading skills

Use the mnemonic VERTIGO to improve your reading skills.

Vocabulary. Being unable to recognize the meaning of words will slow you down considerably, although context and inference can provide cues as to meaning. You can read faster if you know more words. Build up your vocabulary by following these rules:

1   Read widely. The more knowledge you have the easier it is to acquire more.
2   Learn some of the common Latin and Greek roots. Study common prefixes and suffixes. A prefix is one or more syllables added at the beginning of a word to qualify its meaning, while a suffix is added at the end. For example, in the word 'premeditated', 'pre' meaning 'before' is the prefix, 'meditate' means to think, and 'ed' is the suffix which refers to the past tense. Similarly the word 'phobia' means fear. Thus 'claustrophobia' means fear of enclosed spaces and 'hydrophobia' means fear of water. Other phobias include 'acrophobia' – fear of heights, 'photophobia' – abnormal sensitivity to lights, and 'xenophobia' – fear of foreigners. Word analysis or breaking a word into its component parts, as above, is a useful strategy to adopt for understanding words without referring to a dictionary.
3   Watch out for new words. Record them on cue cards for reference. File the cards alphabetically and review periodically. Alternatively, carry them with you and review during spare moments of the day. As you commit the words to long-term memory destroy the cards.
4   Use the new words you learn at every available opportunity. Integrate them into your normal everyday conversation and thereby commit them to long-term memory.
5   Compile a glossary of technical terms in your subject or, better still if available, buy one of the specialist dictionaries in your chosen field. Use this approach to build up your technical vocabulary in your specialist subjects.

Eyesight. If your eyesight is bad and affecting your ability to read, then wear spectacles. Amazingly, many people neglect this because of vanity or inertia. During reading sessions rest occasionally and focus your eyes alternately on a near and a distant object. This will relax and rest the eyes and prevent fatigue.

Regression. Stop regressing. Don't go back over words you think you don't understand. More often than not the meaning will become clear because of context and structure as you continue reading. Readers also regress because they lose their place on the page.

Talking. If you find yourself vocalizing, stop. However, there is one exception to this. When you are trying to understand a complex idea it is often a good idea to speak the key material aloud for better impact and retention. Speed up your reading by avoiding subvocalizing structure words. In fact, the faster you read the less subvocalizing you will be capable of doing.

Ideas. Read in thought (idea or concept) units. Increase your recognition span. For example, when next reading the newspaper fix your eyes on the centre of each sentence of a column. With practice your eyes should be able to take in the beginning and end of the sentence automatically. The columnar structure of newspapers facilitates this process. When reading a text chunk words in groups of two or three at a time which is the size of the perceptual span. Good readers attend primarily to the meaning of the text, while poor readers attend more to its surface characteristics.

Guide. Use a visual guide such as your index finger, a pencil or pen. Run it under the line you are reading without touching the page. Vary your speed in line with your purpose and the difficulty of the text as you progress. This technique focuses your attention and thereby improves your concentration. You won't regress due to losing your place on the page. Using the hand as a pacer allows you to see and read groups of words at a time and helps to reduce subvocalization. It adds rhythm to reading, which involves the right side of the brain. Also, two senses are involved, vision and touch, thus increasing your command.

You may also experience slow recovery, the time it takes to move from one line to the next. Consciously speed up your index finger to minimize your recovery time and speed up your reading. Move in one word on each line and read to the penultimate word to take advantage of your peripheral vision. Always maintain an upright but relaxed posture. The desk you are reading at should be of a suitable height. Some experts maintain that the distance between your eyes and the book should be between 15 and 24 inches. Obviously, using a guide is only appropriate for serious reading – for leisure reading the emphasis is on relaxation and enjoyment.

Operating reading speed. Determine your existing speed. If it is average or below there is no reason why you can't improve it by between 50 and 100 per cent without loss of comprehension. Practise reading faster, straight away! Use the daily newspaper for practice sessions. More importantly, apply the rapid reading technique to your study material as appropriate. Compete with yourself. Make each reading a step towards more effective reading.

It is a good idea to improve your reading by practising one of those skills at a time. When you are satisfied that you are proficient in that one move on to the next. By this process you will build up your skills on a gradual but permanent basis. For more effective and permanent learning distribute your practice over a period of time. Remember, practice makes permanent and practice makes perfect.

The MURDER system for reading with understanding

Apply the MURDER system for serious reading from a business or textbook. Murder is a mnemonic which stands for Mood, Understanding, Recall, Detect, Elaborate and Review.

Mood. Create the right mood and environment for reading. Consider actively the subject that you are about to read. Make sure that the physical conditions are right for reading, including intensity of light, ventilation, height of chair and desk, distance of eyes from the reading material and your posture. For proper posture, the back must be straight and the two feet flat on the floor. Put everything else out of view except the book you are reading. This will focus your attention on the task at hand.

Understanding. Concentrate on deep rather than surface learning. Deep learning is intrinsically motivational – readers try to understand the meaning of their reading and the context of new ideas and concepts. On the other hand, surface learning tends to rote learning.

Recall. Actively recall what you have read. Recall at the end of each section. Spend 50 per cent of your time recalling. Write down the recall words and use them to build up your Mind Maps® later on.

Detect. Detect errors in your recall by comparing it with the text. This immediate feedback will help you correct shortcomings in your level of understanding and recall. Feedback combined with corrective action is a vital element of successful learning.

Elaborate. As you read link the text to mental images, previous knowledge and experience. This will increase the effectiveness of your learning and recall.

Review. Review what you need to remember. Do this from your Mind Maps®. Unless you review you will quickly forget. Psychologists maintain that we forget 80 per cent of what we read within 24 hours unless we review. Within a week we have forgotten almost all of what we have read, unless we review. A systematic review plan is essential.

Improved concentration

Concentration is an essential ingredient for successful reading. Without it you will not retain and learn what you have read. Find a quiet place to read, free from noise, distractions and interruptions. Baroque music, like that of Bach and Handel, played in the background while reading can induce relaxation and make your mind alert and improve concentration. The mnemonic DISPOSAL will help you remember the main points for developing powers of good concentration.

Divide and conquer. Adopt a psychological attitude of divide and conquer. Instead of reading a book, read chapters. Instead of reading chapters, read sections and paragraphs. This chunking has the psychological effect of making the task more manageable. Subgoals create motivation and interest.

Instead of problems focus on benefits. The perceived benefits must outweigh the difficulties. What benefits will accrue to you as a result of reading the book? This attitude will create interest and motivate you to read the text. Remember the WIIFM principle – What's in it for me?

Start and finish time. Estimate how long it should take to read. Have a time block for each reading session with a start and estimated finish time – that which can be done at any time, rarely gets done at all. Apply time management techniques to your reading tasks. You may find that your concentration is better at certain times of the day. Read during those times. Remember the span of concentration is only between about 10 and 40 minutes, so demanding many hours of concentration is unrealistic. Take short breaks every 10 minutes or so and longer breaks every hour. Practise building up your concentration stamina on this basis.

Positive self-talk. Attitude is an important aspect of good concentration. We are what we think we are. If you think you can, you will. If you think you can't, you won't. You set your own psychological limits. The ability of the mind to limit the body's achievement is illustrated by the experience of Soviet weightlifter Vasily Alexeyev. In 1976 no one had ever lifted 500 pounds, and Vasily was unable to break that barrier. His trainers overcame this limit by telling him that the bar only weighted 499.9 pounds, revealing only after he lifted it that it actually weighted 501.5 pounds. Once he'd broken his own 500 pound limit, Alexeyev was able to go on to lift 564 pounds. Say to yourself: 'My concentration is very focused. I am totally concentrated. Every day in every way my concentration gets better and better'. Feed this into your subconscious over a period of time so that it becomes part of your mental set. Impaired concentration can be caused by a conflict between will and imagination. The law of reversed effort states that in such a situation imagination will win. Therefore, we must develop positive and constructive use of the imagination to help focus our powers of concentration. Relax and use repetition each day to imprint affirmations and images into your subconscious.

Ongoing recall. Spend up to 50 per cent of your time recalling. Take notes, preferably in Mind Map® form, at the recall stage and use these for review. Adopt the 5R approach: Read, Recall, Review, Relax and Reflect. Generate images for key words as you read, recall and reflect. People remember pictures better than words and visual memory lasts longer than verbal memory. In an experiment with students psychologists found that students who visualized images to go with the sentences scored 40 per cent higher on comprehension than students who read the same story without visualization. Try and visualize models, diagrams and pictures in your mind's eye. With practice you should improve. These exercises bring the right or imaginative side of the brain into play. By using both sides of your brain you will enhance your learning effectiveness. Relax by doing a deep breathing exercise. Sit comfortably with your arms at your sides. Using your diaphragm, inhale slowly through your nose to a count of four. Hold your breath to a count of four. Exhale through your mouth to a count of four. Rest for a count of four. Repeat the exercise a few times. For progressive muscle relaxation, sit comfortably with your arms at your sides. Take a few deep breaths as above. Starting with your feet, visualize a warm orange glow relaxing every muscle in your body as it slowly moves its way up, ending with the muscles in your face.

Specific objectives. Read with a purpose. Specify your learning objectives at the outset and self-test at the end of the reading session. Benchmarking, feedback and control are important aspects of learning. Reading with specific objectives in mind directs attention and facilitates comprehension of relevant information.

Attend to task. Procrastination is the thief of time. Procrastination has been defined as the automatic postponement of an unpleasant task, for no good reason. Two appropriate scientific laws come to mind here: the 'Law of Inertia' which states that a still body tends to stay stationary and the 'Law of Momentum' which states a body in motion tends to stay in motion. So start it now! Do it now! Take a point of view or perspective as you read to enhance your recall. Naturally, in your case this will be the point of view of a person who wants to improve their reading skills. How will the application of these ideas improve my reading skills?

Look for interest. Attention, interest and motivation are interlinked. To improve your attention you must eliminate external and internal distractions. To eliminate external distractions: create a proper work environment, read in a quiet place or with baroque background music, organize your work space, use good lighting and sit in a comfortable chair. To eliminate internal distractions: relax, know your biorhythms and plan your reading accordingly, verbalize and visualize what you want, set specific realistic goals and break them into manageable subgoals. Interest creates motivation. Relate what you read to your experience and existing knowledge. Whenever possible, choose areas in which you have a natural interest. People learn by linking and associating new knowledge to what they know already. The good reader quickly integrates prior knowledge and experience with text information.

Reading approaches

Vary your reading speed with your purpose. For example, note the following types of goal reading approaches and use them as appropriate. Remember the mnemonic SCRIBE to help you recall the methods.

Specific. You may read to research a topic of interest to you or to obtain specific information say for a particular problem or exam question you want to solve. Use the index to guide you to the particular section that interests you, then read the section carefully. This is an example of reading with a purpose.

Critical. Critical reading involves making inferences, assumptions, deductions, interpretations, predictions and evaluations. Critical reading is essential when reading business books. You must learn to discriminate between what is important and what is not. Is it relevant or irrelevant? Is it supported by the argument or not? Apply the higher level thinking skills such as analysis, synthesis and evaluation to the written text. To support your critical reading approach apply a creative reading strategy. Creative reading involves synthesis, integration, application and extension of ideas. It means making the reading your own and getting more out of it than is actually there.

Revision. Revision reading confirms your knowledge and helps you to retain it in your long-term memory. Use the Mind Maps® or patterns for this purpose, and familiarize yourself thoroughly with all the main concepts. Skipping and skimming can be used with advantage here especially when reading texts.

Informational. Additional reading is essential for most subjects to give you familiarity and a broad background knowledge. Reading around your subject will give you different perspectives and a greater insight and understanding of the topic.

Browsing. Lunchtime often presents opportunities to visit a bookshop or library to browse. Browsing can be a very educational, relaxing and rewarding pastime and can form an integral part of your effective study time management system. Look at any texts that interest you. Practise your skipping and skimming techniques as appropriate, reading only those sections which are important to you.

Enjoyment. Of course, we all read for relaxation and enjoyment. As you know, when reading a novel it is not necessary to read every single word to get the gist of the story. Apply rapid reading techniques with effect here, scanning, skipping and skimming as necessary.

Proofreading is one method which is not obviously applicable to a manager's needs. However, a variation on the theme, such as review or check reading, should be your approach on completing a report or letter. Checkread for grammar, punctuation, misspellings, sense and neatness. Does B always follow A and have you demonstrated it? In practice this simple procedure is often overlooked.

Reading different material

Newspapers. Material in newspapers is organized on the basis of an inverted pyramid, with the most important information presented in the first few paragraphs. Overview the newspaper by reading the headlines. Prioritize by interest and determine purpose. Use the 'must know', 'should know' and 'nice to know' approach. Read all the 'must know' material. For 'should know' material, rapid read the first few paragraphs and the last paragraph. For 'nice to know' material, prioritize on an interest basis and skim through the material as relevant.

Books. Apply the SQ3R method – Survey, Question, Read, Recall and Review. Prioritize by interest or need. What chapters or sections are essential to your purpose? Determine purpose on a 'must know', 'should know' and 'nice to know' basis. Vary your reading speed in line with this purpose. You may need to read all the 'must know' material, survey the 'should know' material and skim through quickly the 'nice to know' material.

Business magazines. Overview the list of contents. Prioritize articles by interest or need. Determine purpose on a 'must know', 'should know' and 'nice to know' basis. Read all the 'must know' articles and apply skimming and scanning techniques to the others.

Business correspondence. Prioritize by interest or need. Pre-read to discard, delegate or read for more detail and action. Decide on the response or follow-up activity required.

Reports. The style of reports varies in line with the subject matter. First survey the report to see how it is structured and organized. There may be a lot of background material which is not of immediate concern to you. Second, look for the theme, scope, development of ideas and conclusions by reading the management summary at the start of the report. Third, read the table of contents and examine the appendices. Then read the findings, conclusions and recommendations. If you need to do more in-depth reading preview the report, marking those sections which are of particular significance and which you may need to study in detail. A Mind Map® summary of the report may save you time later when you need to review the content quickly.

Summary

- For better reading use the SQ3R method: Survey, Question, Read, Recall and Review. Some barriers to effective reading were highlighted. The average person has a reading speed of 240 words per minute. By using efficient reading methods this speed can be improved to about 360 wpm with an upper limit of 600 wpm for conventional reading.

- There are seven main ways in which you can improve your reading skills, following the mnemonic VERTIGO:
  - *Vocabulary*. Improve your vocabulary.
  - *Eyesight*. Wear spectacles if you need them.
  - *Regression*. Stop going back over words.
  - *Talking*. Stop talking to yourself and reduce subvocalizing or inner speech.
  - *Ideas*. Read for main ideas. Grasp them in thought units and increase your recognition span.
  - *Guide*. Use a visual guide such as your index finger.
  - *Operating reading speed*. Practise reading faster. Use skipping and skimming techniques as appropriate.

- Use the MURDER system for reading with understanding – **M**ood, **U**nderstanding, **R**ecall, **D**etect, **E**laborate and **R**eview.

- Good concentration makes a key contribution to effective reading skills. The mnemonic DISPOSAL will help you remember the main points for developing powers of good concentration:
  - *Divide and conquer*
  - *Instead of problems focus on benefits*
  - *Start and finish time*
  - *Positive self-talk*
  - *Ongoing recall*
  - *Specific objectives*
  - *Attend to task*
  - *Look for interest.*

- Reading with a purpose is an important aspect of effective reading. The mnemonic SCRIBE will help you:
  - *Specific*
  - *Critical*
  - *Revision*
  - *Informational*
  - *Browsing*
  - *Enjoyment.*

Chapter 7   Use this page to draw your own Mind Map® of this chapter

8 Effective writing

- What is effective arrangement and presentation?
- What are the 4 Cs of good writing?
- How can I keep my writing logical?
- How can I use clear and concise English?
- What are the principles of good report writing?

Managers and writing

Most managers' jobs entail some writing. Every day managers attend to memos, letters, reports and e-mail. Specialists compile detailed specifications and project reports. Writing is therefore a very important aspect of a manager's job. Few managers have any training in the art of writing. It is usually picked up as their career progresses and on a 'need to know' basis. In any field of business writing is important and managers are often passed over for promotion because they are unable to communicate effectively. As a manager you may also need to edit your staff's writing and give advice on layout and composition. The following paragraphs will give you some advice on how to write effectively in a business context.

Arrangement and presentation

Good writing has an introduction, a middle and an end. Break up your text into paragraphs. Use the first paragraph as an overview of what is

131

to come, the middle paragraphs to develop your theme and the final paragraph as a quick summary and conclusion. A paragraph is a group of sentences forming an idea. A good rule is one idea per paragraph. Vary the length of your paragraphs for effect. If a paragraph is too long consider splitting it. There are no strict rules regarding the length of a paragraph. Short paragraphs and even the one sentence paragraph can be used to grab attention.

People like to read things in small chunks. This has a motivational effect and makes the reader feel that he is making progress. Insert a line space between each paragraph for better visual presentation. Paragraphs should be developed and sequenced in a logical order. Paragraphs with common themes should be grouped together under a heading.

The first sentence of each paragraph is the topic sentence, so put your main idea up front. This indicates clearly what the paragraph is about and helps you stick to the point. Now develop your main point by explanation, analysis, illustration and example. Use the last sentence in the paragraph as a linking device to the idea in the next paragraph. Organize the subject matter of your paragraph in a coherent, consistent and concise manner. Points within each paragraph should be consistent with the main thrust and evolve logically and naturally from the ideas presented. Use headings, subheadings, indentations, underlining, listing and numbering of points, as appropriate, to emphasize and enhance your text.

Clarity

Writing is an individual process. Develop your own style. Avoid trite and well-worn phrases which should have no place in good writing. Think in terms of the reader and adapt your style and content of text to the reader's requirements, identity, knowledge, education and experience. If your audience is diverse, think in terms of the lowest level reader. Identify what the reader actually wants and structure your writing to meet those needs. Know your purpose for writing and keep it continually in your mind as you write.

Apply the main rules of grammar and use words in their correct sense. Good punctuation will help to clarify your sense. A good rule is to write and punctuate as you speak. However, most writing needs some revision, so look over your text to eliminate unnecessary words and phrases. Two people can only understand each other if they use words and phrases that belong to good accepted English. Use good sentence construction and clear writing. Know the difference between a comma, a colon, a semicolon and a full stop. Use these with effect to enhance your writing style. As a general principle try and avoid the use of the semicolon as a full stop can do the job just as well.

Logical argument

Accurate identification of the problem, proper analysis and succinct presentation of conclusions are all required for successful professional work. Therefore, your text must be structured and logical. Point B should be developed and follow from point A. Concepts, arguments, ideas and practical implications should be organized and linked in a logical and coherent sequence.

Lengthy, undisciplined, repetitive text containing wild speculation and invalid assumptions will suggest to the reader that little time has been spent thinking about the issues and their implications. Conclusions should be derived logically from the case made. Never assume that points will be inferred from the text. Always explain fully the development, source and reasons for their thinking.

Clear and concise English

Clarity of mind is usually evidenced by both clarity of speech and the written word. On the other hand, a writer's lack of understanding is often camouflaged by verbosity and long-windedness. Precision and clarity of expression will prevent misrepresentation and misinterpretation. Words have different shades of meaning. Be sure to use those which communicate precisely the meaning intended. If you have a choice between a short and a long word, use the short word. Similarly, if you have a choice between a familiar and an unfamiliar word, use the familiar word. The following are some examples of unfamiliar versus familiar words:

Unfamiliar word	*Familiar word*
utilize	use
furnish	give
ascertain	find
purchase	buy
accomplish	do
transmit	send
attributable	due
correspondence	letter

In this context, remember the four Cs of good writing: Clarity, Correctness, Conciseness and Coherence. One-page letters are more likely to be read and digested than two- and three-page letters, so edit out unnecessary words and phrases.

Verbosity

Why use many words when a few will do the job just as well? Avoid clichés. Try to substitute a word for a phrase. The following are some examples of verbose phrases and the suggested shorter equivalents:

Verbose phrases	*Concise phrases*
in the normal course	normally
in view of the fact that	because
in the near future	soon
at the present time	now
in spite of the fact that	although

make a revision	revise
for the purpose of	for
be kind enough to	please

Clarity does not automatically follow on from brevity, although, generally speaking, being brief does enhance clarity. Short sentences can have great impact if used with discretion. As a general rule write more short sentences than long sentences. Bear in mind, however, that you can be too brief. A happy medium is desirable. Therefore, vary the length of your sentences. This puts variety in your style and makes your writing thoughtful, interesting and pleasing to the eye. On the other hand, being long-winded is often synonymous with confused and woolly thinking.

Keep sentences short

Dr Flesch, author of *The Art of Readable Writing*, recommends that the average sentence should be about seventeen words long. If your sentences are therefore more than twenty words long, you should beware. Most readers have to reread long sentences to understand them. Why give your reader more work to do than is necessary? If you tend to write long sentences review your work to see if you can split some of them into two. One point per sentence is generally a good guide.

Experts also recommend that you keep to at least 70 per cent one-syllable words. Readability then is determined by the choice of words used, the length of sentences and the clarity and conciseness of expression. Use everyday English words, if possible, instead of foreign and technical terms. This is not always practical when technical terminology is appropriate, but is nevertheless a good guiding principle.

Adapt an active rather than a passive style when writing, putting the subject of the sentence before the object. Use concrete in preference to abstract terms as this will make your writing easy to understand. The tone in your writing should be conversational, personal, genuine, friendly and direct. Avoid sexist language, euphemisms and tautology. Explain abbreviations as they are introduced in the text. Be as specific as possible. Instead of referring to a foreign car say a 1994 Toyota Carina.

Spelling

Good professionals, as well as being able to express themselves, should also be able to spell. Study the structure of words. Be aware that some words are composed of a prefix, a root and a suffix. Take the word premeditated. The prefix is 'pre' which means before, the root is 'meditate' which means to think and the suffix is 'ed' which is the past tense.

The following words are commonly misspelt:

Correct spelling	*Often misspelt as*
accommodation	accomodation
beginning	begining
competency	competancy
definition	defination
feasible	feasable
interrupted	interupted
relevant	relevent
separate	seperate
successfully	sucessfully

Try to avoid confusing principle with principal, access with assess and so on. Make your own list of problem words which you frequently misspell or confuse with other words. Study and eliminate these mistakes from your life once and for all. Acquire and use a good dictionary and thesaurus to help you in your efforts.

Writing reports

The report should be functional but attractive. A good cover design may be necessary for impact and to activate the reader's interest quickly. The title page should contain, in addition to the title, the date, reference number, classification (confidential, restricted or general circulation) and the name of the person who prepared the report.

A contents list is essential unless the report is very short. It is good practice to number the pages from the start of the report rather than from the list of contents.

The introduction

The introduction to the report should include the terms of reference, a short background to the project, the name of the commissioner and the reasons for the project and the scope and limitations of the study.

A management summary or outline of the contents should be given next, to help the reader understand the gist and major recommendations without having to read the full report. Not only does this impress but also saves the reader a considerable amount of time.

Body of report

The body of the report should give the method of investigation, the general approach adopted, the type of empirical research undertaken, interviews made and information and facts collected. Statistics, models, diagrams and graphs which interrupt the flow of the language of the report should be relegated to the appendices.

Findings and conclusions

If preferred, or if the size of the report warrants it, the body of the report may be divided up into sections with relevant findings, conclusions and recommendations after each section.

The conclusions must be supported by and follow on logically from the findings. The conclusions must be:

- Consistent. Contradictory statements in different parts of the report create a very bad impression and may defeat any chances of implementation.

- Reasonable. If you have ever studied law you will be familiar with the concept of the average reasonable man and what the judge considers this mythical figure would do in certain defined circumstances. It is a mixture of common sense, logic and sanity. Conclusions must comply with this concept.

- Clear. Conclusions must be clear and unambiguous in language and purpose. Clarity of mind is usually expressed in clarity of speech and the written word.

- Concise. Keep your conclusions short and to the point.

Recommendations

Recommendations are the guidelines which the reader must take to successfully implement the findings of the report. These are the pinnacle of the report. The wording and sequence of the recommendations is thus of the utmost importance. The following are a few guidelines which recommendations should comply with:

- Sound. The recommendations, irrespective of their theoretical soundness, must be sensible and acceptable and thus likely to be adopted.

- Well defined. They must be precise and concise to prevent misrepresentation and misinterpretation.

- Itemized. The recommendations are usually categorized and sequentially numbered within the relevant categories.

- Supported. The recommendations must be supported by data and findings in the body of the report or in the appendices.

All statistical matter, graphs, maps, charts, diagrams, supplier quotations and detailed results of systems investigation should be relegated to the appendices. Reference to the appendices must be made in the body of the report to support statements made.

Principles of good report writing

The working principles of good report writing, which we call the three FYs, are:

- Simplify. Keep the words simple, avoid long sentences and the use of technical or in-company jargon, if possible. Where use of the latter is unavoidable either explain each term as it is used in the report, or alternatively, include a glossary of terms at the start.

- Justify. Every recommendation in your report must be corroborated by findings and facts.

- Quantify. It is a sound principle of good report writing that adequate quantification, to support the points made, should be included.

When writing the report adopt the following order. First, write the body of the report. Second, the findings, conclusions and recommendations in that sequence. Third, the introduction. Fourth, the summary or abstract. Lastly, the appendices. These will be numbered. Relevant parts of the body of the report should be cross-referenced to the appropriate appendices. The use of signposts, section headings, subsection headings, paragraphs, underlining and the itemizing of sentences as appropriate is a feature of good reports.

Summary

- Good presentation skills are very important in your work and personal life. The basis of good presentation skills are:

- effective arrangement and presentation
- clarity of explanation
- logical argument
- clear and concise English
- good spelling, punctuation and grammar.

- Good reports will have:
  - a cover
  - a title page
  - contents list
  - introduction and background
  - management abstract
  - body of report
  - findings, conclusions and recommendations
  - Appendices.

Chapter 8   Use this page to draw your own Mind Map® of this chapter

9 Time management

- Why are objectives important in time management?
- What is the difference between efficiency and effectiveness?
- How can I prioritize work?
- What is Pareto analysis?
- Why is planning important to successful time management?
- How can I increase my administrative efficiency?
- What is procrastination?

Objectives

Somebody once said: 'If you don't know where you're going, you're liable to finish up somewhere else'. Objectives concentrate and focus our energies. People climb mountains because they're there. They present challenges to overcome. Therefore objectives are motivational. The mnemonic SMART will help you to remember the key aspects of objectives:

- *Specific*
- *Measurable*
- *Attainable*
- *Relevant*
- *Time bound.*

Specific and measurable

Don't generalize. To be specific write the objective down. Visualize where you want to be and what you must do to get there. What can't be measured is rarely done. If you can't measure it, you can't manage it effectively. Break down your main goal into subgoals and create time budgets for each subgoal. 'Divide and conquer' should be your motto. Life is hard by the yard, but by the inch it's a cinch. Have regard to quality, quantity, time and cost. These factors will help you plan and control your activities. They create motivation and interest and a sense of achievement on the accomplishment of each small step.

Attainable

Goals should be attainable and capable of achievement. Those which are unrealistic and too difficult to achieve become demotivational. On the other hand, goals which are too easy can also be demotivational. They must not be too difficult or too easy to achieve. To be motivational goals must offer a challenge, but should be within your capabilities.

Relevant and time bound

Goals must be relevant to your job purpose and your career. Finally, goals should be time bound. That which can be done at any time, is rarely ever done. Time constraints concentrate the mind. Management by objectives means achieving goals within time targets.

When considering objectives be aware of the difference between effectiveness and efficiency. Effectiveness has been defined as doing the right things while efficiency is doing things right. You could be very efficient and be ineffective at the same time. In large organizations there are often many people doing unnecessary tasks, but doing them very well. With the passage of time some jobs become unnecessary but the person doing the work may not realize this. On the other hand, you could be very effective and inefficient at the same time. You may be doing the right things but your methods may be time consuming and inefficient in the use of resources. Ideally, therefore, you should be both effective and efficient.

Strategic

Objectives are often categorized into strategic, tactical and logistical or operational. Strategic objectives are long term, bounded by a time horizon of more than one year. Sometimes this is called the helicopter viewpoint – the ability to take a broad and longer-term view of your work. Tactical objectives are medium term, bounded by a time horizon of one year, while logistical objectives are day-to-day activities.

Tactical and logistical

Your career goals are strategic objectives which are made up of tactical or subgoals which you must achieve on the way to your strategic goals. Logistical goals are day-to-day targets which you must carry out to achieve your tactical and strategic goals. Each is linked and interrelated to the other. This clarity of vision should help you keep your eye on the main objective. The tasks and activities you do on a day-to-day basis must be relevant to your medium- and long-term goals. Cumulatively they contribute to the achievement of your strategic goals.

Policies

Policies should not be confused with strategic objectives. Policies are principles that guide action. They help you make good decisions when faced with similar circumstances. For example, you may have a policy of taking your holidays late in the summer rather than early. Other things being equal some people like to support home industry when making purchases. Therefore, policies should save you time by helping you make quick decisions when faced with routine situations.

Know your values in life. They will determine the direction and manner in which you spend your time. For example, have you prioritized the place of your family versus your work? Many people focus on their work to the detriment of their home life. Obviously, the ideal situation is to balance the two without damaging either.

Priorities

Some experts categorize work into 'must do', 'should do' and 'nice to do'. The 'must do' is imperative and accounts for about 75 per cent of what we do. The 'should do' is important and accounts for about 20 per cent of what we do. Lastly, the 'nice to do' might be done just in case the boss asks and accounts for about 5 per cent of what we do. You might use this type of philosophy with advantage when planning and prioritizing your work.

Work may also be classified into discretionary and non-discretionary activities. The implications of not doing discretionary work may not have significant consequences for your job. On the other hand, non-discretionary activities are essential and central to your job. Another classification might be prescribed activities by your company, for example, being required to sit on various committees. These are not central to your job purpose but nevertheless you are required to do them. Measure how much time these activities take and see if you can cut down by negotiating your way out of them or delegating them to somebody else.

The Pareto principle

The Pareto system is another approach to classification of priorities. It is named after an Italian economist who discovered that 20 per cent of the population of Italy owned 80 per cent of the wealth. The Pareto principle is also known as the 80:20 rule – the concept of the vital few and the trivial many. Applied to business situations, and stock control in particular, it suggests that 20 per cent of the stock items account for

80 per cent of the value. Therefore, from a financial savings and stock control point of view it will be more advantageous to minimize stocks of these items than any others.

Creditors' invoices may also be distributed in the same fashion. Analysis of one week's invoices might show that 20 per cent of the invoices account for 80 per cent of the value. This might lead to the conclusion that only invoices over a certain value should be checked thoroughly and the rest checked on a sampling basis, thus saving time. In any event errors on the debit and credit side over the long term will probably cancel each other out. The implications of not carrying out a 100 per cent check is not as serious as it seems because of the small value involved and the likelihood of compensating errors.

Cheques and remittances received in the post each morning may follow a similar pattern – 20 per cent of the cheques may account for 80 per cent of the value. If the volume of cheques is large and pressure of work great, then attention might initially be paid to the cheques of high value so that early banking is achieved. During times of high interest rates significant bank interest charges can be saved.

Other areas where this principle can be applied are in space utilization – 20 per cent of the items in a store, because of their size and bulk, may take up 80 per cent of the floor space. Maybe these items could be stored outside.

Debtors' ledger accounts – 20 per cent of the accounts may account for 80 per cent of the value. To maximize cash flow, follow-up activity should be concentrated on the 20 per cent.

With customer complaints, a small proportion of customers may account for 90 per cent of complaints. Do not become side-tracked on these to such an extent that your valuable customers suffer.

In a training session you might find that 20 per cent of the participants make 80 per cent of the comments. In work you might find that 20 per cent of the employees account for 80 per cent of the level of absenteeism.

You may also discover that a small percentage of activities take up a huge percentage of your time. Worst still, some of them may be of the 'nice to do' variety rather than being critical to your job purpose. Pareto analysis has a part to play in many aspects of business life and its application with discretion could save you a great deal of time. When confronted with a long list of things to do remember that maybe only two or three items are vital. Concentrate on these for greater effectiveness.

Planning

Don't agonize – organize, plan and control. Planning and control are known as the Siamese twins of management. Control is needed to check performance against plans and targets and, if necessary, to take corrective action to put performance back on target. Control is an essential part of planning.

Proactive

Plan for the future because that's where you're going to spend the rest of your life. Murphy's Laws are appropriate here: Nothing is as easy as it looks; everything takes longer than you think and if anything can go wrong, it will. So careful planning is necessary. There are two critical ideas related to planning: reactive and proactive. Being reactive is of course the complete opposite of planning. Being reactive means a lack of planning and forethought. Phrases like fire fighting, fire brigade action and crises management come to mind. In practice the reactive mode reigns supreme in business. The opposite is the proactive mode. People who are proactive, think ahead and try to anticipate what can go wrong, set objectives, plan ahead and monitor progress. Such people, in fact, are more likely to manage their time effectively.

Implementation

A plan is of little value unless implemented. Planning saves time spent on execution. Creating a 'to do' list each day and analysing your time over a representative period are essential tools of the trade. Prioritize your 'to do' list at the start of each day and set a time for completion alongside each activity. A Mind Map® might be a good way of doing this. As the day progresses there is a sense of accomplishment as you tick off the jobs completed. At the end of each day, review your list. What activities have you failed to attend to? Why?

Record your time

Don't rely on your memory for a time analysis. Record how you spend your time over a representative period using a time log. This should only take about 5 minutes a day. After the relevant period carry out a factual analysis of your time. It may surprise you which type of activities are so time consuming. Are they necessary? Eliminate unnecessary activities. Are you spending most of your time, as you should be, on the key functions or core responsibilities of your job? On a day-to-day basis for forward planning, use a good desk diary as your time management information system.

Continuous learning and self-improvement

Train and develop yourself to increase your personal efficiency. Read books on decision making, creativity, speed reading, effective memory, writing, communication and problem-solving skills. Learn during waiting time which includes commuting time, queuing time and travel time. Treat these times as opportunities for self-improvement rather than wasting your time. Even while driving you can listen to self-improvement cassettes. Travel time can be an opportunity to catch up on the latest thinking on management. Take a book with you.

Administrative efficiency

Remember Parkinson's Law – work expands to fill the time available for its completion. Unless you set time targets for yourself you will stretch the work to fill the available time. Administrative efficiency starts with you. Organize your desk. Remove clutter and distractions. Do one thing at a time and put finished work out of the way. When handling correspondence remember the four Ds – do, delegate, delay and dump.

Correspondence

Attend to urgent correspondence of a high priority immediately. For a quick turnaround, write the reply on the correspondence received and despatch immediately, but keep a photocopy for your file. Correspondence which could as easily be done by your staff should be delegated. Delay and file for future review and attention anything which is not of an urgent or important nature. With the passage of time some of it may lose most of its significance and may be dumped. A significant proportion of the correspondence may be junk mail which can be also dumped. Someone once said that next to the dog the wastepaper basket was a man's best friend. Some correspondence may refer to other parts of the organization; after a quick perusal redirect for action by someone else.

A lot of time may be wasted by drafting and redrafting letters. The price of perfectionism is prohibitive. While you want letters to be of a good standard and project a good image for your company, it is not necessary to go to elaborate rituals of checking and rechecking to achieve this. Remember the concept of cost benefit analysis.

Managing the phone

Plan your phone calls in advance. Determine the purpose of the call and plan your questions beforehand. Have relevant files and correspondence close at hand for reference. Decide on periods of the day when you will take and make calls. With modern phones you can now record and hold calls for future action during valley periods of the day. Ask your personal assistant to screen incoming calls. Set up an appointments procedure. There are many people who hate to waste time alone. Discourage casual drop-in and time-wasting visitors.

Filing

A good filing system is an important adjunct to administrative efficiency. You should be able to retrieve information quickly. Apply the Pareto principle. You might find that 20 per cent of your files are responsible for 80 per cent of the reference activity. Put these files together. Weed out those which are not referred to frequently and file them separately.

Meetings

Meetings are probably the greatest time consumer of all. A committee has been described as a group of people who keep the minutes and waste hours. Do you need to be present at the meeting? Do you need to be present for all of the meeting? Can you delegate attendance to a member of your staff? Ask the chairperson at the start of the meeting how long it will take.

How much time is allocated to each item on the agenda? Bear in mind the saying that the time spent on any item on the agenda will be in inverse proportion to its value. There is a tendency to spend a disproportionate amount of time on the trivial. Make sure that this does not happen and that items are prioritized and allotted time in relation to their importance. This will concentrate participants' minds on priority and time management. Also be aware that the length of a meeting increases in proportion to the number of people present. Chairmanship skills are essential to keep everybody's contribution on target.

Delegate

Surveys show that managers are often reluctant to delegate. They take comfort in absorbing themselves in routine tasks. Some do not trust their staff. Others fear that they will be held responsible for mistakes made by their staff. They may have the attitude that by the time you show staff what to do you could have done it yourself. This is very short-term thinking.

Of course, delegation assumes that you have the staff to delegate to and that they are able, willing and trained to undertake the work. Remember, jobs which are routine to you may present a challenge to staff. Part of your job as a manager is to train and develop your staff. Giving them increased responsibility and more demanding work is an excellent way of developing them. It also frees you to concentrate more on your managerial role.

Procrastination

Procrastination is the thief of time. Procrastination is putting off until tomorrow that which you should attend to today. Plan a definite time for the completion of your tasks. Remember time is money. Work out how much you cost per hour. This is only about half of what you really cost if you were to take overheads into account. Are you giving your company value for money? We all have only 24 hours in a day and 168 hours in a week. You can't borrow time, hoard time or earn more time. You can only invest time, spend time, organize time and waste time. Drucker says time is the scarcest resource that managers have. Make better use of your time than anybody else by careful planning and prioritizing.

Management

The functions of management are planning, organizing, controlling, leading, motivating, delegating, communicating and coordinating. Are you skilled in these areas? Improve yourself by reading books and attending training and development courses. Develop computer expertise such as keyboarding skills, word-processing, e-mail, graphics and spreadsheet skills. These will enhance your personal productivity. Delegate routine tasks to staff and coach them to take on more demanding work. Do not interfere in the staff's own area of discretion. Never tell staff how to do things. Tell them what to do and they will surprise you with their enterprise and ingenuity.

Summary

- Objectives should be SMART – Specific, Measurable, Attainable, Relevant and Time bound. They should be broken down into subgoals with time targets set for each.
- Prioritizing is important. Classify activities as 'must do', 'should do' and 'nice to do'. Tackle obviously urgent and important jobs first.
- Plans must be implemented to achieve objectives. Proactive means thinking ahead, while reactive is a complete absence of planning. Make a factual analysis to ascertain how you spend your time.
- Administrative efficiency can increase your personal productivity and improve your time management.
- Procrastination is putting off till tomorrow what you should do today.
- Good management skills will help you do your job more effectively and in less time.

Chapter 9   Use this page to draw your Mind Map® of this chapter

10 Presentation skills

- What are the four Ps of good presentation?
- What are the ingredients of a good plan?
- How should I structure my presentation?
- Why is body language so important?

Introduction

One of the greatest fears in life is that of public speaking. One survey found that it was even greater than the fear of death. Most of us, whether we like it or not, will occasionally speak in public. Indeed if you want to get ahead in your career, good presentation skills are essential. A survey of middle and upper managers found that the ability to communicate ideas and plans effectively in front of an audience was ranked the number one critical skill for managers who wanted to progress in their careers. Three-quarters of those surveyed considered it three times more important than writing skills for career advancement.

You can learn much about presentation skills by reading and observation, but to become really proficient in public speaking you must take every opportunity to practise. The four essentials of good presentation skills are *Planning, Preparation, Presentation and Postmortem*.

Planning

The following verse by Kipling will provide a structure to help you remember the key elements of good planning when making presentations:

> I keep six honest serving-men
> (They taught me all I knew);
> Their names are What and Why and When
> And How and Where and Who.

The most important question is Why? Some novices focus entirely on technique and forget about why they are making the presentation in the first place. What is the purpose or objective of the presentation – to persuade, inform, motivate, entertain or teach? Basically you want your audience to listen, understand and be influenced by what you say.

Keep them interested

If you want your audience to listen you must make your presentation as interesting as possible. Conversational tone, anecdotes, metaphors, quotations, examples, illustrations and visuals will enhance your presentation and make it more memorable. If you want your audience to understand what you're saying you must have regard to their interests, needs, point of view, and existing level of knowledge. Tailor your message to suit the audience and keep it simple. If you want to influence your audience, you must show how your presentation will benefit them. Use logical argument to support your case. Emphasize benefits rather than features. The objective will influence the design, structure and approach of your presentation.

Who is your audience?

Who is your audience going to be? Why have they come? What is their age, gender, experience, education and level in the company? What are their hopes, needs, interests, attitudes, expectations, concerns and fears? What do they want to know? What do they know about the topic already? Are there any special considerations you need to address? The answer to these questions will influence the content, style and level of your presentation. So think about and research your audience in advance in order to make a good presentation.

Check out the room

Where will the presentation take place? Check out the room in advance. Make sure the layout, seating, lighting, electrical sockets, heating, ventilation and equipment are suitable. There are many traps for the unwary; a thousand things that can go wrong. Remember that seating arrangements – horseshoe style, classroom style, conference style etc., – will impact on your presentation. Some seating arrangements facilitate interaction and participation, while others discourage it. Which style will facilitate your purpose?

Know your equipment

Familiarize yourself with the equipment and know how to operate it without creating distraction and fuss. At the minimum when using an overhead projector make sure you know where the on/off switch is. Depending on the make, it may be located at the front, rear or side. To guard against Murphy's Law – If anything can go wrong, it will! – make sure you have a spare bulb and that you know how to fit it. For extra insurance have a standby machine available. If possible, rehearse your presentation at the venue beforehand. If this is not possible, a mental rehearsal is almost as good. In any event, arrive at the venue ahead of schedule to check that everything is in order.

When does it happen?

When will the presentation take place? How long will it take? If you have a choice, morning time is the best. People are generally at their brightest and sharpest in the morning. Trainers regard the afternoon as the graveyard shift because people are tired and drowsy, a condition which is often compounded by a heavy lunch. Remember that the average concentration span is at the most about 20 minutes. In a long session it is a good idea to use audience participation every half hour or so, by allowing sufficient time in your plan for questions and answers. Use overheads, flipcharts, discussion and questions as appropriate. Put variety into your presentation. Generally the longer it is the more variety of approaches you need. Allow time for mid-morning and mid-afternoon tea and coffee breaks of between 10 and 20 minutes' duration. Good presenters always start and finish on time.

How are you going to make your presentation? Will you stand behind a podium or without any physical barriers between you and the audience? Some experts are of the opinion that physical barriers create psychological barriers and thus detract from your presentation. What visual aids are you going to use? What equipment do you need?

Research your subject

What will be the subject of your address? Where will you obtain the information for it? You may be able to draw on your own experience in combination with research inside and outside the company. However, bear in mind that if you are going to stand in front of people they expect you to know what you are talking about. Anticipate possible questions and research appropriate answers beforehand. Make sure you know and understand your subject. Have sufficient interesting material to fill the time allotted to your presentation. After all you are projecting yourself as the expert! Do not disappoint your audience.

Preparation

All good stories have a beginning, a middle and an end. Good presentations are exactly the same. Overview – tell the audience what you're going to tell them and the purpose of your presentation. Inview – tell them. Review – tell them what you've told them and what actions they should undertake as a result of the presentation. Occasional repetition of key concepts will help maximize the impact and facilitate audience retention of your message. Stick to this little formulae for effective presentations. If you want audience participation, use open questions like What? Why? When? Where? How? and Who? to generate discussion and involvement.

Seven main headings

Preparation is the key to success. The structure, sequence and logic of your presentation is all important. Most experts maintain that you should organize your thoughts under not more than seven main headings. These main headings can be used to organize subheadings which again should be kept to not more than seven points. Mind Maps®, which were discussed in Chapter 6, are a great technique to help you brainstorm and marshal ideas. With the recency/primacy principle of memory in mind make your opening and closing as memorable as possible and counteract the sag in the middle by the use of rhetorical questions or other methods of audience involvement.

Mind Maps®

Mind Maps® will drastically cut down on planning and preparation time. They concentrate on main ideas and discourage you from learning entire presentations word for word. They will give a natural flow to your talk, while facilitating eye contact, informality and logical organization. One Mind Map® sheet may substitute for many cue cards. Cue cards sometimes fall out of sequence at the worst possible time causing much embarrassment and distress to the speaker. Mind Maps® are imprinted on the mind during their preparation because of their unique format so that recall and review is facilitated. Some people can visualize the Mind Map® and mentally walk through it without reference to notes during their presentation. However, this requires much confidence and practice and is not recommended for the novice.

Visual aids

These days a presentation is incomplete without the use of visual aids. People are used to seeing effective presentations on television backed by stunning colourful graphics. As a result they now demand and expect good presentations. Consider your material on a 'must know', 'should know' and 'nice to know' basis. Prioritize the 'must know', be frugal with the 'should know' and ruthlessly eliminate the 'nice to know' material. Remember your audience is only likely to retain about seven key points. Why detract from and clutter your main message by side-tracking on peripherals?

Most people prefer to keep the technical side of making presentations simple by mostly relying on the overhead projector with transparencies. OHP transparencies are relatively easy to use and inexpensive to produce. Hence the reason for their popularity. Despite the advances in information technology the use of multimedia with computers should be left to the expert. They can still be cumbersome and malfunction at the worst possible moment and may thus distract from rather than enhance the speaker's performance.

With modern computer graphics there is no excuse for poor quality visuals. OHP transparencies should be well designed with a large, punchy, colourful message. Limit your points to six per transparency with a maximum of 20 words. Don't forget to check the spelling. Participants often think that presenters who misspell words are stupid! Create contrast between text and background to improve readability. Many transparencies lose their impact because they contain too much information. People can't absorb a lot of information in one go. In fact, key points might warrant a transparency for each point to focus and emphasize the message. Always maintain eye contact with your audience. Don't stare at and talk to the transparencies. When using a flipchart do not turn your back on the audience.

Presentation

You have planned and prepared your talk and now you are ready for the big event. It's a good idea to greet people as they enter the room. Introduce yourself to each person and ask them to introduce themselves to you. This breaks the ice. Most people imagine that the content of the presentation is very important. However, studies show it accounts for only 7 per cent of the impact, whereas your physical presence can account for 55 per cent and your voice for the remaining 38 per cent. Remember that you exude confidence through your voice, posture, eye contact and gestures, therefore content is not the most important factor. The speaker's appearance and delivery are much more important. This gives you an idea of the importance of non-verbal communication, sometimes called body language. It's not what you say as much as how you say it. How can you use body language to enhance your presentation?

Eye contact

Eye contact is possibly the most important aspect of body language. The eyes are the mirror of the soul. When speaking scan the audience with your eyes while occasionally making eye contact with the odd member of the audience. Eye contact should only be maintained for a few seconds. Avoid staring – it can make people feel uncomfortable.

Use your hands

Use your hands to emphasize your points. When not in use keep them at your side in relaxed mode. For obvious reasons never adopt the figleaf or reverse figleaf position. Putting your hands in your pockets is also not recommended. Study how good public speakers move their hands and use them as role models. Gestures to emphasize points should flow naturally from the topic and not be adopted robotlike.

Watch your mannerisms

Are you aware of any inappropriate mannerisms that you may have developed unconsciously? Obvious examples include rattling change in your pocket, pacing up and down like a caged lion, fiddling with pencils or glasses and using vocal fillers such as 'ums', 'aas' and 'you know like'. Ask a close friend to give you honest feedback in this area so that you can take corrective action. Work on one fault at a time. Remember to stand in a stationary position, with your feet about 18 inches apart and well balanced. A relaxed posture is essential to the art of effective presentation.

Smile!

Smiling is contagious. A smile relaxes you and your audience. A smile says 'I'm friendly, I'm happy to be here and I like you'. So smile! It sounds easy, but how many public speakers have you seen smiling? The self-fulfilling prophecy suggests that if you adopt a positive and friendly attitude towards your audience, they will respond in kind. Build up a rapport with your audience. People will eventually forget what you said, but they'll remember how you made them feel. We are led by our heart rather than our head.

Be enthusiastic

Develop a passion and enthusiasm for your subject. Believe in what you say. People become vibrant when they talk from their own convictions and interests. If you're not interested in your topic, how can you expect the audience to be? Remember as many names as possible and use them during your presentation. Use the rhetorical questioning approach. Occasionally call upon one or two participants for their views on some issue. This is a great attention getter and keeps others on their toes as well.

Listen

When handling questions from the audience listen empathically, with your ears, eyes and heart. Many people concentrate on formulating what they're going to say next rather than listening with understanding to what is being said. Listening with your eyes means that you observe a person's behaviour. Communication experts maintain that most of what we say is communicated by body language. Listening with your heart means listening for feelings. Participants bring their own emotional baggage with them – uncertainty, doubt, joy, sadness, anger, prejudice, hostility, confusion, resentment, frustration, pride, loyalty, etc. A good presenter will try to empathize with the audience, to get into their shoes and understand their point of view.

Use your voice effectively

Your voice is the musical instrument you use to put your message across and keep your audience interested. Use tone, pace, pitch (inflexion), pause and volume to modulate the impact of your message as appropriate. Tone refers to the characteristics of a sound. One person's voice may have an essentially different tone from another. Adopt a friendly relaxed conversational tone.

Slowing your speed can emphasize a point. On the other hand, speaking quickly may give a sense of urgency or excitement, provided you still articulate properly. Pitch is a musical term. It refers to how high or low a note is, or in this instance how high or low your voice is. In general, you should start sentences in a low pitch and finish in a higher pitch. Changing pitch gives colour and variety to your voice. Continuous high pitch can create the impression that you're nervous. On the other hand, continuous low pitch makes you sound tired or depressed.

Pause before an important point to heighten expectation and focus attention. This also gives the audience an opportunity to digest what you've said. However, a pause of more than 4 or 5 seconds may sound as if you are lost for words. Volume is a measure of how loud a sound is, how to make yourself heard without shouting. Project your voice so that you can be heard at the back of the room. Raising the volume can also be used to highlight a point. A sudden drop in volume can command attention. Mumbling and ending sentences on a lower volume is very annoying to the listener. Speaking to an audience is not the same as speaking to one person.

If you are using a microphone for the first time make sure that you practise in advance to eliminate the novelty and self-consciousness involved. There is nothing worse than sitting through a presentation where the speaker drones on in the same monotone throughout the performance. Such an event can be sleep inducing.

The four Cs of good presentation

The four Cs of good presentation are to be Clear, Concise, Concrete and Colourful.

Clear. Being clear means that you can be understood. Speaking up and good pronunciation are essential. Good grammar is important too. Remember the KISS mnemonic – Keep It Short and Simple! Avoid jargon and complicated words and phrases.

Concise. Keep your sentences short, relevant and to the point. If you are long-winded people will have forgotten the point by the time you reach the end of the sentence. The Fogg index suggests that most people have difficulty understanding long sentences. A suggested maximum length to facilitate comprehension is between 15 and 20 words. However, do vary the length as short snappy sentences can have great impact. If you want to be understood, keep them short.

Concrete. Research shows that concrete words are understood faster and remembered better than abstract words. Keep your words concrete. Call a spade a spade.

Colourful. Paint word pictures and visual images with your words. Appeal to the emotions. Use illustrations, anecdotes, examples and humour as appropriate. Remember one of the greatest public speakers of all time, Jesus Christ, used parables to illustrate complex moral and religious themes.

Postmortem

Feedback on your performance will help you to learn from your mistakes and to take corrective action to eliminate faults. Continuous improvement should be your objective. You must develop a sensitivity to the needs, wishes and reactions of your audience. During the presentation be aware of your audience's body language which should tell you whether you are holding their concentration and interest. Indicators such as looks of boredom, yawns, clock watching, puzzled looks, fidgeting, glazed over eyes, wriggling in seats and uneasiness should be acknowledged and your performance adjusted to sharpen up the presentation.

If you are giving a training session study the post evaluation sheets to see what reaction the participants had to your presentation. Reflect on your performance and determine to improve next time. Analyse your presentation – what worked, what didn't and why?

Remember there is no one right way to make a presentation. The great communicators build on their unique style and personality. Some of them even go against conventional wisdom. Developing your own style will enhance your presentation Like any other skill the art of effective presentations must be learnt. All you need is plenty of practice. Use it or lose it.

Summary

- The four Ps of a good presentation are Planning, Preparation, Presentation and Postmortem.

- The questioning approach – Why? What? When? Where? How? and Who? – will help you to plan effectively.

- Preparation is the key to success. A good presentation will have an introduction, a middle and an end.

- Mind Maps® will help you to structure your thoughts.

- More so than content the use of body language can make or break your presentation.

- The four Cs of good presentation are to be clear, concise, concrete and colourful.

- Finally, for continuous improvement of your presentation skills you need feedback on your performance.

Chapter 10   Use this page to draw your Mind Map® of this chapter

11 Interpersonal relationship skills

- Why are communication skills so important?
- What is non-verbal communication?
- What is the communication model?
- What are the barriers to effective listening?
- How can I improve my human relations skills?
- How can I make a good impression on others?

The importance of human relations

Human relations skills are much more important than technical skills if you want to become a senior manager. Good communication is a very important aspect of interpersonal relationships. Listening is one part of communication which sounds fine in theory but is rare to find in practice. Empathy will help you to understand people and respond to their needs more effectively. Understanding the basic communication model should help to improve your communication skills. Experts maintain that as much as 65 per cent of the message communicated is non-verbal or body language. There are some practical tips you can apply to help people to like you more.

Communication is two-way

Communication is the art of sharing ideas, information, instruction or feelings. The basic ingredients of good communication are clear thinking, clear speaking and clear writing. We spend about 75 per cent of our waking hours in some form of communication such as talking, listening, reading and writing. That's a lot of time. It makes sense to do it effectively.

There are 1 million words in the English language (about 200,000 of them are technical). The average person has a recognition vocabulary of 10,000 words and a conversation vocabulary of 2000 words. However, in everyday usage most people manage on a vocabulary of as little as 300 words. In everyday conversation therefore, you should choose words that are most frequently used and understood. It is also wise to keep sentences short and to the point. Avoid jargon and 'in-company' phrases, particularly when dealing with outsiders such as suppliers and customers. All large organizations develop their own jargon; fine for those on the inside, but confusing for those on the outside.

Listen to learn – learn to listen

The average speaking rate is 175 words per minute, but we think at about 400 words per minute. This gives each of us a lot of spare capacity for mental doodling. Try to counteract this natural phenomenon by concentrating on what the speaker is saying and meaning. Focus on central ideas rather than details. Use your spare mental capacity for summarizing main points, anticipating what is going to be said and observing body language.

Concentrate

Experts in communication estimate that only about one-quarter of all listeners are able to understand the main idea when listening to a speaker. If you find your mind wandering when listening to somebody, you must get back into focus. You can use the spare capacity (the difference in speed between speaking and thinking) productively. It makes good sense to summarize in your own mind the key concepts and ideas the speaker is trying to convey. If you're unsure about the message, be brave and repeat it back to the speaker's satisfaction. This is called feedback and ensures that two-way communication has taken place. Remember, communication does not take place until it is understood. Speaking quickly and indistinctly may also prove a barrier to communication.

You are now beginning to realize that communication is not as easy as it seems. We talk, listen, read and write each day but we don't give it much thought. However, we must continually work at each of them if we are to become skilled in that most underrated art – communication.

Ask questions. Ask, don't tell. Use open-ended questions. Questions beginning with Who? What? Where? When? How? and Why? In dealing with enquiries we need to elicit information in order to identify and solve the problem. So use this questioning technique.

Effective listening

Have you ever been at a meeting where nobody seems to listen to anybody else? Of course, you have. The meeting consists of a series of monologues. The people are not really listening to each other, but thinking and planning what to say as soon as the other person pauses for a breath. Experts maintain that the best way to make friends is to become an attentive listener. Many people fail to make a favourable impression on others, simply because they do not take the trouble to listen. Communication is a two-way process and listening is a very important aspect of it. Somebody once said that the reason we have two ears and only one mouth is because we should listen twice as much as we talk. Apart from anything else, it is just plain good manners to listen. The next time you are in conversation with someone, lean a little forward to show your interest and be seen to be actively listening and eager to help. Consider some of the barriers to effective listening. The mnemonic WASTAGE may trigger off the critical points:

Wishful thinking. Most people only hear what they like to hear. This phenomenon is known as wishful thinking. Any sort of criticism, no matter how constructive and legitimate, is filtered out and falls on deaf ears.

Attention. Don't permit your thoughts to stray or your attention to wander. Focus your mind on what the person is saying. Practise shutting out outside distractions and concentrate on what is being said. Listen for ideas and meaning, not just words. We want to understand the whole picture, not just isolated bits and pieces. Develop an enquiring mind.

Semantics. This is the science which deals with the development of the meaning of words. Do not put an interpretation on words and phrases other than that intended by the speaker. Seek out the meaning by questions, discussion, clarification and feedback. Avoid words, phrases and jargon which the other person is unlikely to understand.

Talk person to person. Don't be too formal. Be sincere and sympathetic in your manner. Build trust. Never breach confidence. Make the other person feel welcome and important. Use the little courtesies, which unfortunately these days seem to be going out of fashion, such as 'Good morning', 'Please', 'Thank you', 'Would you mind', 'Would you be so kind as to' and so on. They make life more pleasant. Watch for and respond appropriately to non-verbal signals. As well as concentrating on what is being said, study the body language accompanying the message.

Attitude. Develop a positive attitude to others. Don't close your mind to other people's opinions and viewpoints. There are enough 'know alls' in the world without you joining their ranks. Show respect for their opinions. Don't consider yourself too good to learn from others. Pride is one of the seven deadly sins. Don't fear improvement, correction or change. Listen, you may learn something.

Get the facts. Don't prejudge a person or situation. Many people stereotype others by their nationality, colour, race, religion or appearance. Listen, understand and then judge. Don't jump to conclusions. Find the facts and stick to them. Don't infer things in addition to those stated.

Excessive talking. How many of us are infatuated with the sound of our own voice? We cannot listen and talk at the same time. Comment on what the speaker is saying without interrupting the flow. Occasionally paraphrase what you hear. This provides vital feedback and ensures that the message is being received and understood.

Empathy

Are you a sensitive person? If not, then you must try and do something about it. Sensitivity is probably the most important factor in successful communication. Sensitivity in a nutshell is the ability to see things from the other person's point of view. The North American Indians had a saying, 'You are my friend when you walk in my moccasins', which captures the essence of sensitivity. Empathy, which means listening with understanding, is the modern expression for the same idea. Colleagues, managers, customers and suppliers are people. People have feelings, opinions, fears and prejudices. Empathize with them and show concern and respect. People like to be appreciated and made to feel important – don't you?

Self-awareness

Self-awareness is a key factor in good personal relationships. Be aware of your own strengths and weaknesses. Optimize your strengths and minimize your weaknesses. You must become aware of your personal biases, likes and dislikes and shortcomings. If they are interfering with your social skills, then you must eliminate them from your behaviour. Before you develop the ability to cope with others, you must first have the ability to live with yourself. Keep your emotions under control. Be cool, calm and collected. Never lose your temper with others. Remember, the best way to win an argument is to avoid it and the best way to cook your own goose is with a boiling temper!

There is an old Chinese proverb: 'Man with sour face should not open shop'. Yet how many times do we go into shops to be met by unsmiling, uncaring and disinterested faces. It doesn't cost anything to smile. A smile says, 'I like you', 'I am glad you're here', 'I'm glad to be of service'. When you meet people, do you smile? Develop a sense of humour. Don't take yourself or life too seriously. Learn to laugh at yourself. However, don't laugh at others and avoid sarcasm at all costs.

Are you responsive to others? Listen and accept the feelings content as well as the word content of the message. Listen and question for facts, feelings and opinions so that you have a total understanding of the message. Be positive. Tell the person how you propose to solve the problem and the action you will take with a specific comeback date.

The communication model

In the basic communication model there is a sender, a message and a receiver. In other words; a speaker, words and a listener.

Sender

First the sender (speaker) conceives an idea which must be formulated or translated into words. The effectiveness with which the speaker conveys the message will depend on choice and appropriateness of words, vocabulary, tone and gestures. All these factors help to project the message with precision and clarity. The message may be distorted, ignored or misunderstood, if any of these is mishandled by the sender.

Message

The message consists of words and non-verbal cues. What are words? Words are symbols which represent concrete objects and concepts. It is important to remember that words can create understanding and inspire people to great deeds or they can create misunderstanding, distrust, annoyance and bad feeling. So pick your words with care and discretion.

Words are not necessarily the precision tools of description that they are made out to be. For example:

- *Words mean different things in different contexts.* In the context of a training programme, 'course' means curriculum, but in the context of a horse or a greyhound race it means route.

- *Words mean different things in different cultures.* When Danny Kaye was told his act 'went a bomb' in London he was insulted. In the US this means a flop.

- *Words mean different things to different people.* A bull to a farmer means livestock. On the other hand, to a stockbroker, it means a person who buys shares in the belief that the price will rise so that they can sell them and make a profit.

Receiver

The third ingredient in the communication model is the receiver. The involvement of the receiver can be considered in three ways. Firstly, the receiver recognizes what the speaker is saying and tunes in. Secondly, the receiver interprets the meaning of what is being said by mentally summarizing and reorganizing the idea. Thirdly, the receiver understands the message which has been assimilated, associates and consolidates with existing stores of knowledge and only then responds to what has been said. You can now see just how complicated communication is. Mishaps can occur at any stage and interfere with the message.

This is the communication cycle. Well almost! To be effective communicators, you should use the technique of feedback before you respond with your own opinions to what the speaker has said. How do you do this? Simple. Just practise the following rule: Do not respond with your own feelings, evaluations or opinions until you have first restated the ideas and feelings to the speaker's satisfaction. Practise this rule and you'll be surprised how often you will change your opinions in a discussion or argument. It will take the heat out of the exchange. It will make you more constructive and less critical, because you will be less interested in scoring points and more interested in solving problems.

Verbal and non-verbal communication

The experts tell us that only 35 per cent of what we mean is in the verbal message, i.e. in the words we have chosen to convey our ideas. The other 65 per cent of the meaning is contained in the non-verbal part. Facial expressions, in particular those of the eyes, and other body movements must be considered when interpreting meaning. In any social interaction with other people you must be aware of the non-verbal cues and signals. Psychologists have been paying increasing attention to these non-verbal aspects of communication. The following are some of their findings. The mnemonic BAD FUN will help you remember the points.

Boredom. The hand over mouth to cover a stifled yawn can mean boredom (or just a late night). Glances at watches, frequent recrossing of legs, constant repositioning on seat, fidgeting and eyes wandering can also indicate boredom, disinterest, impatience or tiredness.

Arms folded. Folded arms usually indicate resistance; the listener is forming a protective barrier against you and your ideas. But beware, it can also mean other things.

Disbelief. Scepticism or disbelief is often shown by the sharp corner of the eye look that flashes between adjacent listeners.

Frown. The frown may suggest disagreement, lack of understanding or annoyance. Several responses are possible. You can back up and restate your last point. You can pause and ask for questions, or ask if you can clarify your point.

Upward glance. Watch people's eyes. The eyes are the mirror to the soul. The 'skyward glance', eyes cast up towards heaven, may mean 'Dear God, here she goes again' or 'I've heard that one before'. Eye contact is essential for good communication.

Nods. Some people habitually nod or shake their heads slightly as they agree or disagree with what's being said. This will give you some idea whether your listener is agreeing or disagreeing with you. A nod on your part will let people know that you agree with them. Don't assume that they know how you feel. Nod your head in agreement as appropriate.

Body language

So words in themselves only give you part of the meaning of the message. Keep your eyes open. Sharpen your powers of observation. In your dealings with colleagues, management, customers and suppliers watch for non-verbal communication, such as:

- *Facial expression*. Facial expression tends to show emotion and level of interest and thus regulates the conversation. Is the person friendly, angry or disinterested looking? Lack of eye contact, blank stares and yawns may indicate lack of interest. Adapt your approach in line with the non-verbal feedback.

- *Gesture*. Movements of the hand can emphasize a point made or indicate annoyance or impatience. Certain gestures are associated with good manners, courtesy and diplomacy. A firm handshake is associated with confidence and credibility. Scratching and nail biting may be signs of nervousness. Of course, there are also other types of gestures to indicate opposition, hostility and anger. Read and interpret these signs.

- *Posture.* Body stance can tell us a lot about people. Slouching can be a sign of indifference, poor morale or apathy, but it can also be just a matter of poor carriage. People who like each other often stand near each other with relaxed postures. Walking tall indicates confidence, whereas those who walk with a stooped gait are seen as lacking in confidence.

- *Tone of voice.* Tone of voice is influenced by volume, rate, pitch, expressiveness, accent and diction. 'I didn't like her tone of voice'. How many times have you passed this remark or heard others saying it after an encounter with someone you thought was overbearing, pompous, cynical or patronizing? Listen for overtones and undertones. An overtone is a subtle addition to the main meaning, whereas an undertone is a hidden or suppressed feeling.

Memory

The average person has a poorly trained memory. Both the long-term and short-term memories are important factors in communication. Research has shown that we forget 50 per cent of what we read immediately unless we review. We forget 80 per cent of what we hear within 24 hours. We forget 90 per cent within 48 hours and another 90 per cent of the 10 per cent we remember within a week. 'So what?' you may ask. Well, it highlights the importance of writing down enquiries which you cannot attend to straight away, particularly in the case of telephone calls. Don't rely on your overworked memory! If you cannot handle the enquiry immediately, record (full details, name, address, telephone number etc.) for subsequent attention. It also highlights the necessity of maintaining reminder systems, such as desk diaries and brought forward filing systems. A well trained memory is a valuable asset.

Encouraging people to like you

We all want to be popular and liked, not only in our social relationships but also in our working relationships. But how many of us are prepared to take positive action to help us achieve this goal? Getting along with managers, peers, suppliers and customers is a most important aspect of your job. Teamwork is essential to the satisfactory conclusion of work tasks. You need people at work and elsewhere for occasional help and support. You must impress others favourably so that they work on your side.

There are some practical steps we can take to encourage other people to like us better. We can put the following tips into practice straight away:

- *Own concept of self.* Many books have been written about the power of positive thinking. The problem with negative thinking is that it becomes a self-fulfilling prophecy. The good news is that positive thinking is likewise a self-fulfilling prophecy. Shakespeare said: 'There is nothing good or bad except that thinking makes it so'. Believe in yourself. Think positive experiences. Think about your successes rather than your failures. Develop a mindset for success. Positive expectations are more likely to lead to positive outcomes. Positive thoughts precede positive actions and positive actions produce positive results. Negative expectations are more likely to lead to negative outcomes. Positive thinking is about developing a favourable image of yourself. Remember there is often little correlation between success and a positive self-image. Many successful Hollywood stars have a very negative self-image and commit suicide. Unless you have a favourable image of yourself you cannot impress others favourably. You must be able to like yourself before you can like other people. Develop faith in your own ability to handle colleagues and bring work tasks to completion. The more successful you are the more confident you will become in the future. Don't underestimate yourself and never sell yourself short.

- *Show interest.* Take a genuine interest in the people around you and in the work environment. To be interesting, be interested. Ask questions that the other person will enjoy answering. Encourage them to talk about themselves and their achievements. Disraeli said: 'Talk to a man about himself and he will listen for hours'. Develop a friendly and helpful attitude. Always try and be sincere. If you are artificial, people will eventually see through you. Be positive. If you don't know something, say: 'I don't know, but I'll certainly find out and let you know', rather than a curt: 'Don't know'. Develop a reputation for reliability. If you say you're going to do something, do it!

- *Remember to smile.* A smile is like a piece of sunshine. You'll be surprised at the friendly way people will react. Smiling facilitates positive thinking by giving you a psychological lift. You can't smile and entertain negative thoughts at the same time. Develop a cheerful disposition.

- *Name.* People like to hear the sound of their own names. One of the best ways of creating goodwill is to remember names and use them. To remember names, relate them to the person's features and repeat the name frequently during the conversation.

- *Manners.* Good manners are a sign of good breeding. Manners help make living pleasant. Like smiling, good manners cost nothing but reap many benefits.

- *Learning is a lifelong continuous process.* Seek out opportunities for self-development, not only in your work life but also in your personal life. Action cures fear. Don't procrastinate. Undertake that educational programme now – whether formal, such as certificate, diploma or degree programmes, or informal, such as challenging recreational pursuits. It will make you a more interesting person.

- *Practise.* Practise the previous advice. It's like driving a car, if you practise these, they will become automatic confident responses. Bernard Shaw once remarked: 'If you teach a man anything, he will never learn'. Learning is an active process. We learn by doing. Only knowledge that is used sticks in your mind.

Some experts maintain that the ability to handle people is three times more important than technical expertise in determining the suitability of people for senior managerial positions. So all the technical knowledge (or job knowledge) in the world is of relatively little use if you aspire to senior management, without the social skills to handle people.

Handling people

The following guidelines will help you to handle people. Remember the mnemonic TRESPASS:

Tact. Don't argue. The best way to win an argument is to avoid it. Let the other person do most of the talking. Use the feedback technique. Ask questions in a friendly voice. Use the open-ended questioning technique – Why? What? When? Where? How? and Who? Arguing encourages emotional responses such as anger. Anger leads to irrational behaviour and anything that encourages anger should be avoided. If, despite everything, a person gets angry, don't get angry back. 'Anger blows out the light of reason, but, after a roaring hurricane expends its fury, the lull of calm sets in.' Let the angry person blow themselves out.

Respect. Show respect for the other person's feelings and opinions. Tact and diplomacy are the watchwords here. Never say directly, or suggest to a person, 'You're wrong'. You could say: 'You may be right, but let's look at the facts'. Nobody likes being told directly that they're wrong, especially in front of a third party. Lord Chesterfield said to his son: 'Be wiser than other people, if you can; but do not tell them so'. You may praise but never criticize in front of others. If you use diplomacy and tact, they may admit to themselves that they are wrong. But never, if you crudely try to ram the fact down their throats.

Empathize. See things from the other person's point of view. How would you feel if you were in their shoes? That is what empathy means. Think ahead and try and anticipate reactions. Henry Ford said: 'If there is any one secret of success it lies in the ability to get the other person's point of view and see things from his angle as well as from your own'.

Simple. Speak in simple language. Remember the KISS technique – Keep It Short and Simple. Avoid jargon or technical terms. Don't try to impress others by using big words. Always use the simple word in preference to the long word. Keep your sentences short. Big words and long-winded sentences amount to woolly thinking, confusing others as well as yourself.

Praise. Most people are very reluctant to praise others, even when it is due. We spend most of our time knocking others. Treat people as winners and they will live up to your expectations. A sincere compliment for work well done is a boost to morale and an incentive for sustained excellence in the future. 'You can always catch more bees with honey than you can with vinegar.' However, insincerity is counterproductive. If you criticize for whatever reason, always soften the criticism with praise first. Criticize the act not the person.

Appeal to senses. Dramatize your ideas and involve the other person. Appeal to as many of the senses as possible – hearing, sight, taste, smell and touch. When making a presentation to a group use visuals – a picture speaks a thousand words. Remember the old proverb: 'I hear, I forget; I see, I remember; I do, I understand'.

Synchronize with your listener. Watch for body language and non-verbal communication. Try and synchronize your words with the speed of receptivity of the listener (you can gauge this from the actions and expressions of the listener). Mirror your body language to that of the other person.

Sell. Make the other person feel the idea is theirs. This is the best way to implement your ideas. Use the open-ended questioning technique to obtain viewpoints. Concentrate and develop those on which there is common ground and agreement. Show what's in it for them. Most people are motivated by self-interest.

Making an impression on others

The mnemonic PLEASE may help you to remember the critical points about making an impression on other people:

- Posture
- Look, listen and learn
- Expression
- Appearance
- Speech
- Eagerness to help.

Posture. Your posture can indicate clearly whether or not you are going to be friendly and helpful. Indifference, nerves, restlessness and lack of confidence can all be indicated by posture.

Look, listen and learn. For the total message listen for the words and observe the accompanying body language. Pay attention to what they say and show that you are really interested in them. People prefer to talk about themselves, rather than listen to you. Don't interrupt the speaker or change the subject or you will show lack of interest and may create resentment.

Expression. Most people look at your face, and particularly your eyes, at some point during your conversation. Shakespeare said that the eyes are a mirror of the soul. Remember, your face and eyes reveal your feelings. They show the other person not only how you yourself feel – tired, interested, uninterested – but also how you feel about the other person. It's polite and a sign of attentiveness to look at the person who is talking to you (but avoid staring). Looking at a person also gives you an opportunity to notice their expression. Use your mouth. A smile, especially when greeting someone, can be the biggest ice breaker of all. Your mouth can show friendliness as easily as it reveals boredom and hostility.

Appearance. When somebody comes up to you, both you and your work area are on view. Do you give the impression that you are friendly, neat, well-groomed, smart and organized? Remember, if you look untidy, your work may be untidy too! People act on impressions. Make sure that you are neatly turned out and look after your appearance and personal hygiene.

Speech. Your first words create an impression which colour the other person's reply. If they are friendly and positive, they invite a smile and a thank you from the other person. Nothing is more annoying than unhelpful, negative remarks. Remember to use the person's name. There is nothing sweeter to a person's ear than the sound of their own name. Use the name frequently during the conversation. Link some outstanding feature with the person's name to remember it better. To be heard and understood, you need to speak clearly and look at the person as you speak. Do not use bad language or slang in conversation. If you use bad language you will let yourself down and people will judge you by the way you speak.

Eagerness to help. Adopt a positive attitude and helpful manner in your dealings with people. Show in a positive way that you are enthusiastic, eager and willing to help solve problems. If you want to make friends you must be seen to be obliging, unselfish and thoughtful.

Summary

- Communication is a two-way process. It does not take place until it is understood. The communication model is a three way process consisting of a sender, a message and a receiver. The barriers to effective listening are highlighted by the mnemonic WASTAGE: Wishful thinking; Attention; Semantics; Talk person to person; Attitude; Get the facts; Excessive talking.

- Non-verbal communication is very important. The mnemonic BAD FUN will help you recall some of its key aspects: Boredom; Arms folded; Disbelief; Frown; Upward glance; Nods.

- Some important guidelines for handling people were discussed and can be recalled by the mnemonic TRESSPASS: Tact; Respect;

Empathize; Simple; Praise; Appeal to senses; Synchronize with your listener; Sell.

- The critical points in making a good impression on others can be recalled by the mnemonic PLEASE: Posture; Look, listen and learn; Expression; Appearance; Speech; Eagerness to help.

Chapter 11   Use this page to draw your own Mind Map® of this chapter

12 Stress at work

- What is stress?
- What are the symptoms of stress?
- What are the effects of stress?
- What are the sources of stress at work?
- How can I manage stress?

What is stress?

Stress can be thought of as an individual's response to threats and challenges in the environment. It is not the events themselves but how we view them that causes stress. It can be manifested psychologically or physiologically or both. People who are experiencing stress feel a threat to their self-esteem or their ability to cope and feel tired, anxious, irritated and overworked. Stress is not only negative. A certain amount can be motivational and helps us work to our peak performance.

People have different stress tolerance levels. Some find certain situations a challenge while others find the same situations stressful. Some occupations are more stressful than others. Without stress in our lives we would find living very boring. Worry is a great source of stress yet research shows that 98 per cent of our worries never materialize. It is the way you react to and handle stress which determines whether it is good or bad. An accumulation of stressful events may eventually break the camel's back. There are preventive maintenance strategies which you can adopt to counteract stress.

Sources of stress at work

Sources of stress at work can include work overload, work underload and poor relationships with your manager and peers. Examples of the latter are personality clashes, misunderstandings and breakdowns in communications. Conflicting demands on time, conflicts of interest, interdepartmental conflicts and responsibility for people may also be stressful. Other sources include long hours, shift work, excessive travel, poor working conditions, noise, lack of job satisfaction, threat of redundancy, boring repetitive work, frequent change, alienation, lack of involvement in the decision-making process and lack of control over your job. In times of recession with little possibility of external opportunities and little internal promotion people often feel trapped in their jobs. Threat of redundancy creates more aggression in workers, who become overprotective of their jobs.

Job-personality fit

People whose backgrounds, education, aspirations and interests are incompatible with their jobs have what industrial psychologists call a bad 'job-personality fit' and often live in a perpetual state of stress. The problem seems to be one of unfulfilled expectations. They may be overqualified or underqualified for a job. Either can be a source of stress. If you're overqualified you can always seek promotion or a more responsible job elsewhere. If you're underqualified you can undertake training or better still a formal academic or professional qualification. The Peter Principle suggests that people are promoted until they reach their level of incompetence. If this is true, there are a lot of stressed executives in business.

Some managers are stress carriers

Many managers display little understanding of the psychology of handling people even though the higher up the hierarchy you go the more important interpersonal relationship skills become relative to technical skills. In fact some managers are stress carriers. They pride themselves in their ability to create stress for their staff instead of creating a stress-free environment. Policies of job enrichment, job enlargement and job rotation may help empower and improve job satisfaction and reduce potential sources of stress. Having responsibility without the concomitant authority is a main source of stress in many organizations. Role conflict, role ambiguity and role incompatibility also give rise to stress and strain on the job.

Role conflict

Role conflict happens when a person who is acting in several roles simultaneously finds that the roles are incompatible. A businessman receives a phone call, during a very important meeting, from his wife who wants him to come home because of some domestic problem – he will experience conflict in his role as businessman and family man. Similarly conflict may be experienced by a working woman who is trying to reconcile the demands of a career with those as a mother. Many married men in a dual working situation do not realize their wives are no longer a social support system. They need to do their share in an equitable partnership and recognize the changing role of men and women in modern society.

Role ambiguity

Role ambiguity arises when either an individual is unsure of his role, or some members of his role set are not clear what his role is. Role ambiguity may be because of a lack of clarity about the responsibilities of the job, although a job description may help to remove the uncertainty. There may also be a lack of clarity about how performance is evaluated and how promotion is achieved.

Role incompatibility

Role incompatibility occurs when different groups, such as management, government and trade unions, have different expectations about what an individual should be doing. These expectations may also differ from the individual's own role expectations.

Role overload and role underload

Work overload leads to burnout. On the other hand, work underload leads to rust-out. Work overload can be rectified by good time management, planning, goal setting and delegation. Having too little to do can be just as stressful as having too much to do. Having too little responsibility, with too little stimulating work creates feelings of low esteem and makes people feel frustrated, underused and undervalued Stress affects all workers, but the middle management and lower-level employees are the worst affected. The least stressful is probably the chief executive's job. The chief executive has reached the apex of Maslow's hierarchy of needs and thus has become self-actualized. He has ultimate control in the decision-making process, whereas middle management and lower-level workers may have insufficient control over the decisions which affect their lives. The less control people have over their work lives the more stress they will suffer. Political leaders whom one would expect to live lives of great stress usually live to a great age. New technology in the workplace is also a source of stress. Computers can cause eyestrain, headaches, frustration, shoulder and arm pains.

Restructuring programmes

Many companies are implementing cost reduction strategies by reorganizing, re-engineering and downsizing to cope with competition and rapidly changing markets. There is much emphasis these days on delayering, participation, empowerment, multiskilling, part-time working and subcontracting. Middle management in particular often find that their jobs are under threat. Senior managers can now obtain information directly from their screens without the assistance of middle management. In the slimmed down organizations the remaining staff have more work with greater responsibility and demanding deadlines. There is thus greater stress on people to perform and achieve results. Change should only be introduced slowly after full consultation with all concerned. Uncertainty and lack of communication is a prime source of stress.

Cost of stress

The cost of stress at work can be quite considerable and is often hidden. It can be seen in the rate of absenteeism, staff turnover, poor morale, low productivity, inferior quality, poor job performance, industrial sabotage and antisocial attitudes and behaviour at work. However, work is not the chief source of stress. In the Holmes-Rahe Scale of stress ratings work occupies only two spots on the top ten items of stressful life events, the other eight relate to personal areas of life.

Effects of stress – psychological

Psychological responses include depression, apprehension, self-doubt, forgetfulness, poor motivation and concentration. Unreleased built-up tension can contribute to health problems such as high blood pressure, coronary heart disease, peptic ulcers, hypertension and cancer. So it pays to combat stress, not only in work but also in your lifestyle generally.

Excessive anxiety has adverse effects on work performance. People under high stress are less able to tolerate ambiguity and to distinguish the trivial from the important. Their approach to work becomes disorganized and they are prone to make more mistakes. They are also more accident prone. A certain amount of stress or anxiety is normal. It keeps the adrenalin flowing and may in fact sharpen your concentration powers, thereby improving the quality of your work performance.

There is obviously an optimum level of anxiety. A high level is stressful, hinders concentration, intellectual control and work performance. A low level is unstimulating and causes lethargy. This has been recognized in the psychological law called the Yerkes-Dodson Law, which states that anxiety improves performance until a certain optimum level of arousal has been achieved. After this point performance deteriorates.

Effects of stress – physiological

In prehistoric times, when life was less complicated, man coped with stressful situations by means of the fight or flight response. In modern times this response is usually inappropriate resulting in an increase in tension without any mechanism for release. Bodily responses include increased heart rate, shortness of breath, trembling hands/legs, palpitations, nausea, perspiration, pallor and in some cases even fainting. Physical signs, such as increased heart rate and blood pressure, fatty deposits in the blood and perspiration, can be measured scientifically. High levels of anxiety can also cause sleeplessness, headaches, aches and pains, muscular tension, lack of appetite, listlessness, stomach pains, even vomiting and reduced immunity to infection. More serious disorders such as peptic ulcers, hypertension and coronary disease are also linked with stress.

Stress management strategies – Work

Creative visualization

You can mentally train for your work situations by doing work successfully in your own imagination. Rehearse in detail in your mind the steps involved as a dry run. Psychologists have found this practically as good as doing the real thing. Athletes use creative visualization in addition to their normal physical training to enhance their overall performance. For example, it is an important aspect of a professional boxer's training. So use your imagination in a positive rather than a negative way. The anticipation of a stressful event can give rise to more anxiety than the actual experience of the event. Students find that taking exams is not as bad as anticipating them because you haven't time to worry. Therefore, control over your imagination will reduce the level of your anxiety. Remember the saying that many a trouble would break like a bubble if we didn't rehearse it and tenderly nurse it.

Time management

By developing good habits such as time management, planning, goal setting, delegation, problem solving and decision making, effective reading, effective writing, memory, mind mapping and presentation skills you will help to optimize your performance and reduce stress. Prioritize your work and don't procrastinate. Good managers must be able to balance their work, home, time and tasks.

Flexi-working

Working arrangements such as flexi hours and flexi place (working occasionally from home) and teleworking (working strictly from home) are modern developments which may help create job satisfaction and alleviate stress at work. Functional organizations tend to be bureaucratic and territorial. Managers build empires as power bases and tend to defend any attempts to erode their positions. In modern business jobs are dramatically changing but organization structures are sometimes out of phase with the change.

Be assertive

Don't take on more work than you can cope with. Some people are afraid to say 'No'. If you take on too much the overall effectiveness and quality of your work will suffer. You may think you're indispensable, but in reality your job is easily filled when you're sick or, indeed, dead.

Strengths and weaknesses

Analyse your strengths and weaknesses. Exploit your strengths and acknowledge your weaknesses. Surround yourself with competent staff who can compensate for your weaknesses and complement your strengths.

Set realistic goals

Setting yourself the goal of becoming a professional basketball player if you are only five feet tall would certainly be unrealistic. Similarly, if you are very tall it is unlikely that you would make a successful jockey. Have regard to your strengths and weaknesses when setting goals, not only in your work life but also in your personal life. Your goals should be specific, measurable, attainable, realistic and time bound.

Training

Your mind needs exercise just like your body. Keep up to date. Undertake training programmes to upgrade your skills and even degree courses in your specialization to keep your knowledge up to date and your mind sharp. Learning is a lifelong process. People become brain dead if they don't challenge themselves mentally on an ongoing basis. Courses in stress management, assertiveness training, presentation skills, time management, interpersonal skills and counselling are some of the topical courses available to help you combat stress.

Stress audit

Some organizations carry out stress audits to gauge the job satisfaction and mental health of their employees. The Occupational Stress Indicator is a questionnaire which helps to identify sources of stress.

Social support systems

We all need friends, both inside and outside the workplace, to discuss our worries and concerns with. Problems with family, finance and friends can be an important source of stress, and to handle it effectively we need the support and understanding of our family and friends. Some progressive organizations operate employee assistance programmes to help staff cope with stressful situations in the work place and also in the personal, financial and domestic parts of their lives. They now realize that it pays to have a happy and contented workforce.

Success first time around in whatever you attempt will reinforce your confidence, optimize stress and motivate you for subsequent success. Nothing succeeds like success. Have long, medium, short and immediate term goals. Subgoals create feasible, quickly realizable steps which act as immediate motivators. Little successes create the proper positive mental set and thus build up your confidence.

Stress management strategies – mental approaches

Models

Find out how successful executives cope with stress in the workplace. Use them as models to modify your behaviour and control your stress levels. People learn by modelling themselves on the successful coping strategies of others.

Desensitization

You must learn to face up to your fears and problems. There is an old Irish saying which says that if you run away from a ghost it will continue chasing you, but if you confront it, it disappears. Before any stressful situation, such as public speaking, think of the issues which are likely to cause you anxiety. Now imagine yourself dealing with each of these issues successfully and conclusively in a cool, relaxed and competent fashion. Rehearse this creative visualization in conjunction with a relaxation technique over a period of time. When the actual event comes round you will behave in a less anxious way. You have learned a relaxed, comfortable association with a situation which previously caused anxiety and even panic.

Positive thinking

Avoid self-preoccupation and negative thoughts. Concentrate on your successes rather than on your failures. Think of ways in which problems can be solved and difficulties surmounted. Treat problems as potential opportunities. Think positively and constructively. Practise positive self-talk rather than negative. Negative self-talk lowers performance and increases stress. Positive self-talk has the opposite effect. Shakespeare said: 'There is nothing either good or bad, but thinking makes it so'. Rehearse in your mind through creative visualization positive experiences of past successes and other achievements. Keep a balanced perspective. Life is not all about work; it's about enjoyment too. Remember, don't take life too seriously as you'll never get out of it alive!

Stress situations

Learn to recognize the situations which cause you stress and develop coping strategies such as positive thinking, desensitization and relaxation. Avoid those situations by using forethought. For example, you can avoid traffic congestion by leaving earlier in the morning for work.

Laughter is the best medicine

Develop a sense of humour. Laughter often provides new perspectives on stressful problems. Laughter is therapeutic. Research suggests it can relax nerves, improve digestion and help circulation. It can increase the body's level of endorphins which improve resistance to disease. Learn to laugh at yourself and at life. Try to see the humorous side to life. Keep things in perspective.

Persistence

You have no chance if you give up too easily. Remember it is often the persistent plodder who succeeds in the end, rather than the brilliant person. Develop powers of willpower and determination. Enjoy utilizing your willpower and doing your best to be successful at work. Say to yourself: 'My willpower keeps getting stronger. I enjoy using my willpower. It feels good to give it my best shot'. So stick to the task. Remember the little prayer:

> Let nothing disturb thee;
> Let nothing afright thee;
> All things are passing.

God alone never changes.
Patient endurance attains to all things.
God alone suffices.

Confidence

Confidence is a belief in one's ability. It is the expectation of a successful outcome. Build on your success. Nothing succeeds like success. Failure situations should be avoided. Success reinforces the expectation of success and lays the foundation for further achievement. However, confidence must be backed up by planning, goal setting, enthusiasm and hard work.

Learn right-brain skills

In a dynamic work environment the ability to be imaginative, innovative, creative and have the capacity to adopt changes quickly and smoothly is all important. Reliance on left-brain skills, like memorized job routines, is no longer sufficient where new methods and technology are continuously being introduced.

Concentration

Concentration is focused attention or strong thinking activity directed at a limited area so that other areas are simultaneously shut out. Build a wall of concentration around you. Concentrate on the here and now, forget about the past and future. Get lost in the present. You want to shut out everything except the item under consideration. You must become so absorbed in what you are currently doing that you become completely unaware of all other potential distractions. Think about the task rather than about yourself. You can improve your concentration through positive self-talk, such as: 'I'm beginning to concentrate'. 'I'm concentrating fully' and 'my mind is crystal clear' will condition the mind in the appropriate way.

Motivation

Executives are motivated by the three Rs – recognition, responsibility and reward. People crave recognition. Everybody should be made to feel like winners. People like their contribution to the organization to be visibly recognized. Executives like the freedom and autonomy to make their own decisions. Salary increases and bonuses are always welcome.

Stress management strategies – lifestyle

Relaxation

Use techniques such as meditation, massage, breathing exercises, autosuggestion, biofeedback and progressive relaxation methods. Progressive relaxation works by sequentially tensing and relaxing your muscles from head to toe. Adopt a comfortable sitting or lying position for these tension reducing exercises. Various forms of breath control can be practised anywhere to reduce stress. A well known breathing exercise is taking a deep breath, holding it and then breathing out – in the ratio of 1:4:2. This simple exercise reduces stress by optimizing oxygen and carbon dioxide levels in the blood. If you want to pursue these ideas further there are many books and cassette tapes available on relaxation techniques in your local bookshop. Listening to your favourite music can also be a great way to unwind and induce a state of relaxation, or sitting in a comfortable chair while conjuring up a mental picture of a relaxing scene such as a view of the sea. Concentrate on the scene. Imagine you are actually there. Live and feel the experience.

Health

Sleep, exercise and eating wisely are all ways of keeping a sound mind in a sound body. Smoking and drug abuse are out, while alcohol can only be recommended in strict moderation. In fact, it is now claimed that the occasional drink is good for your health. Vigorous exercise will help you sleep soundly and a balanced, varied diet with adequate fibre will combat stress and fatigue. Physically fit people are able to cope with stress better than those who are unfit. Medical evidence shows that there is a positive correlation between physical fitness and work performance. Vitality, stamina and a high tolerance level for stress are some of the benefits of being physically fit.

Some medical experts recommend that you should drink eight glasses of water a day (dehydration thickens the blood while hydration thins it) and reduce your salt intake as part of any stress management programme. Salt tends to increase the harmful effects of stress while vitamin C tends to lower it. Therefore, it is suggested that people in stressful occupations should lower their intake of salt and increase their intake of vitamin C. Make sure that you have at least eight hours regular sleep. If you can manage on less you are exceptional.

Leisure time

A good recuperative antidote to the stress of work is to fill your leisure time with plenty of physical exercise. Doctors have found that high stress levels, as measured in cholesterol concentrations, high blood pressure and blood clotting rate, all decrease significantly when a person exercises regularly. Exercise is available to all and costs nothing, whereas approaches like transcendental meditation and yoga are available only to the relatively few. 'All work and no play makes Jack a dull boy'. You need to have a balanced life. Two thousand years ago Plato said: 'Anyone engaged in mathematics or any other strenuous intellectual pursuit should also exercise his body and take part in physical training'. If your work is sedentary, the ideal leisure pursuits should be outdoors with plenty of fresh air and reasonably energetic in order to counteract lack of physical activity. Some psychologists feel that your leisure time should be sufficiently different and challenging to provide alternative stress. This should occupy your mind totally so as to distract you from thinking about work-related problems. If you're skydiving it's hard to be preoccupied with problems at work as well. Some executives undertake outward bound training programmes as a way of creating alternative stress. Leisure activities should be built into your programme as a way of rewarding and reinforcing good work behaviour.

Behaviour types

The medical profession has now identified a particular type of person who is prone to stress and the related health risks, the A type. The person who follows a more moderate and less stressful existence they have named the B type. Type A is always in a hurry (hence the term, hurry sickness), forever trying to meet deadlines. They have feelings of great time pressure and impatience. Type A is very competitive, always has to win and tends to be reactive. They tend to habitually work late and take work home. Type B, on the other hand, is more methodical and proactive, is just as ambitious but works in a less aggressive but nevertheless systematic purposeful manner. Type B is good at planning, has developed good work practices and is aware of and applies good time management techniques. Research has indicated that many chief executives are in fact type B persons. Type A persons don't live long enough to become chief executives.

Type B has established correct priorities, practises good time management and as a result achieves the same goals with less hassle and energy output than the frenetic nervous output of type A. It has been established that type A is more prone to a host of illnesses, including stomach ulcers, cancer and heart disease, than type B. Although the A and B classification is thought by some to be too simplistic, nevertheless, it is a useful model for guidance as to less stressful behaviour styles.

From a work point of view, some of the stress management strategies outlined will help you to be more successful in your job. Furthermore, they will prolong your life and establish a more healthy stress-free lifestyle for your future. If you want to live a long, happy and healthy life then model your behaviour on the type B person.

Summary

Unmanaged stress lowers attention, concentration and intellectual control. Managed stress, on the other hand, can maximize your work performance. Stress management strategies, which can be used to counteract and control work stress, include:

- desensitization
- physical exercise
- positive thinking
- relaxation
- creative visualization
- lifestyle
- having realistic goals
- training
- developing social support systems.

Chapter 12   Use this page to draw your own Mind Map® of this chapter

Mind Maps®

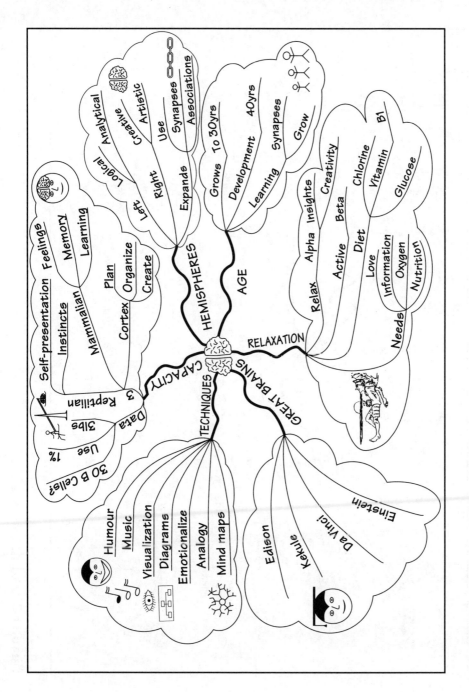

Chapter 1 How the brain works

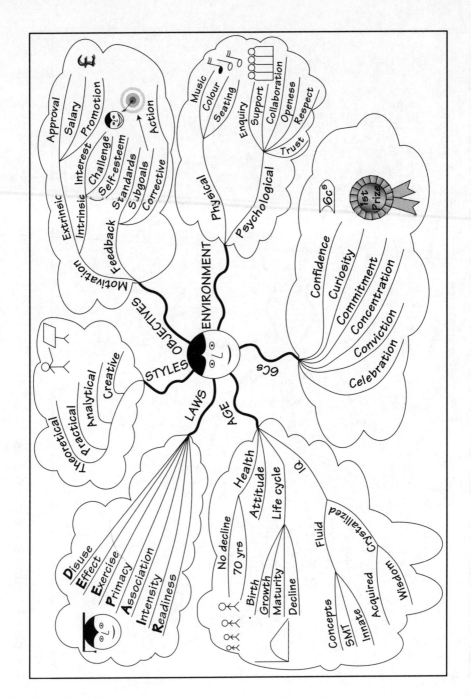

Chapter 2 Adult learning skills

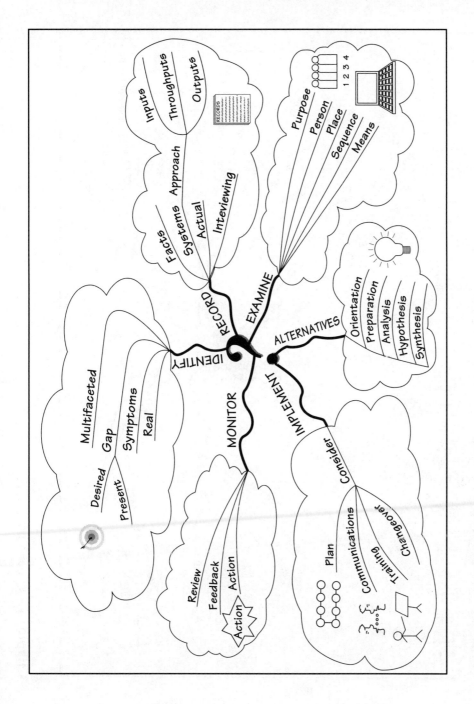

Chapter 3 Problem solving

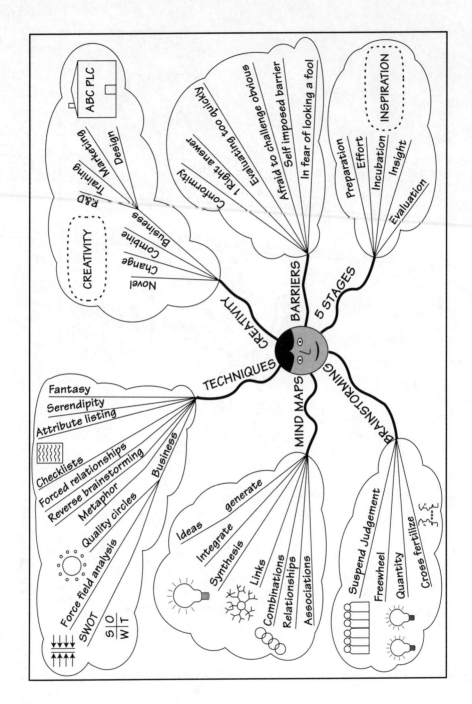

Chapter 4   Creativity

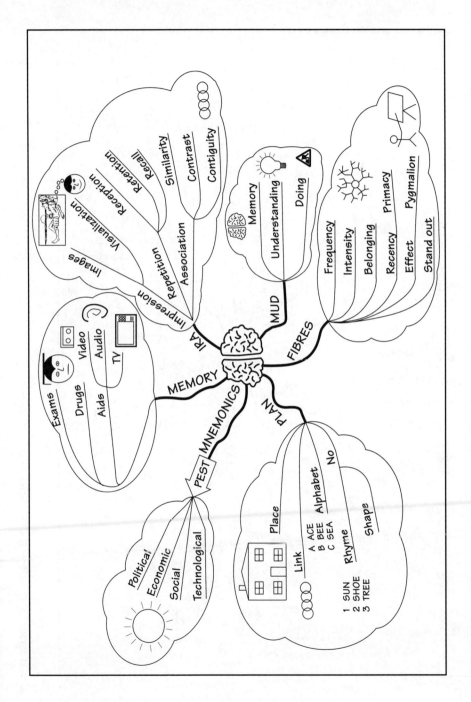

Chapter 5 Effective memory

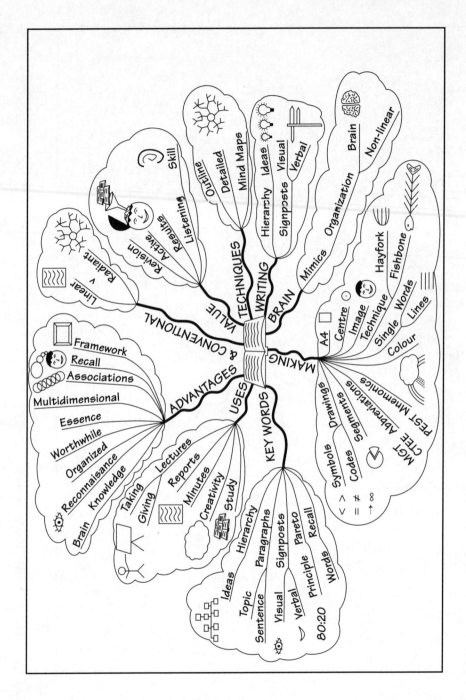

Chapter 6 Note-taking and Mind Maps®

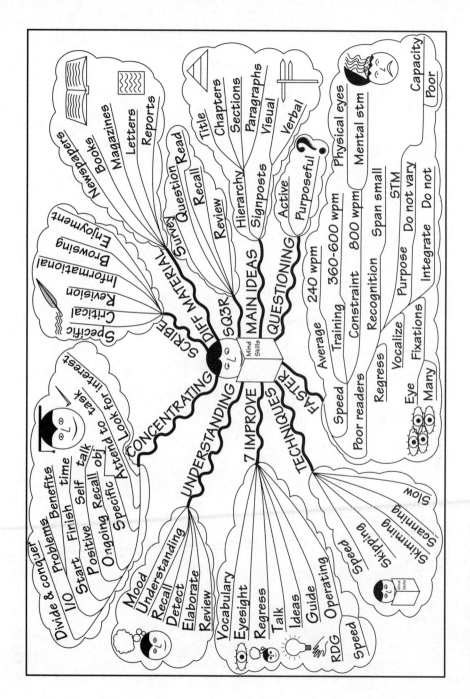

Chapter 7 Effective reading

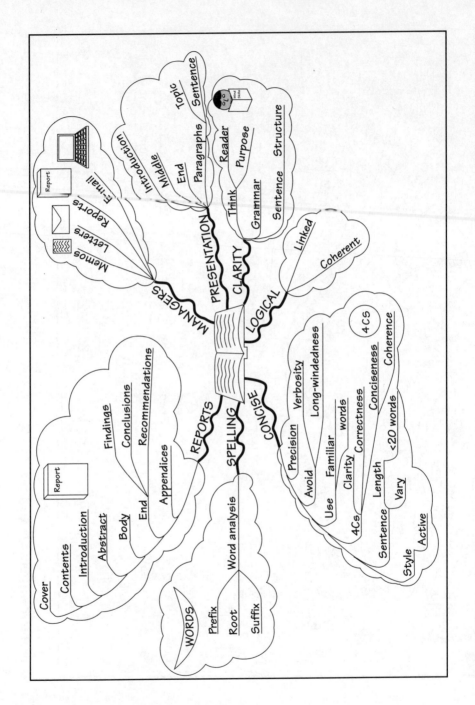

Chapter 8 Effective writing

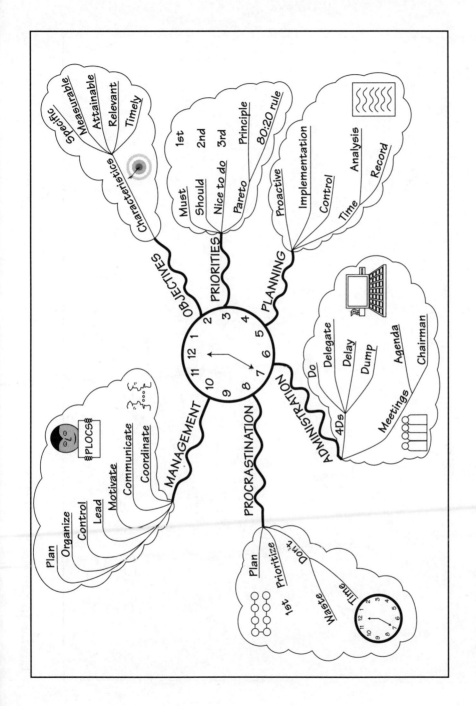

Chapter 9   Time management

Chapter 10 Presentation skills

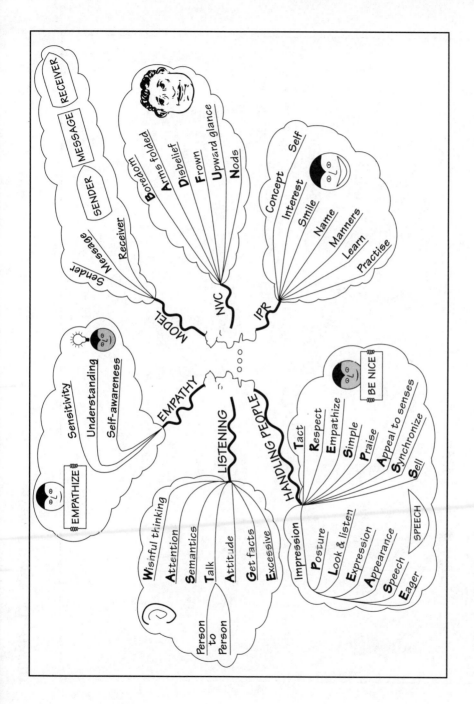

Chapter 11 Interpersonal relationship skills

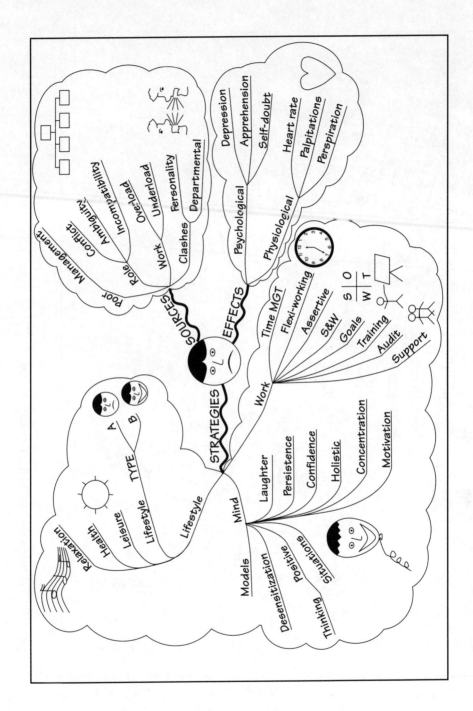

Chapter 12   Stress at work

Bibliography

Adair, John. 1985. *Effective Decision-Making*, London, Pan Books Ltd.

Adair, John. 1988. *Effective Time Management. How to save time and spend it wisely*, London, Pan Books Ltd.

Agardy, Franklin. 1981. *How To Read Faster And Better*, London, Angus & Robertson Publishers.

Anderson, Joseph V. Jan. – Feb. 1993. 'Mind mapping: a tool for creative thinking' in *Business Horizons*, pp. 41–66.

Baddeley, Alan D. 1993. *Your Memory. A User's Guide*, London, Prion, Multimedia Books Ltd.

Becker, Dennis and Becker, Borkum Paula. 1994. *Powerful Presentation Skills*, New York, Business One Irwin/Mirror Press.

Becker, Stephen P. April 1978. 'Learning contracts: helping adults educate themselves' in *Training HRD*, vol.15, 4, pp. 57–9.

Bliss, Edward C. 1976. *Getting Things Done. The ABC Of Time Management*, London, Futura Publications.

Blythe, Peter. 1975. *Stress The Modern Sickness*, London, Pan Books Ltd.

Bobbert, Dr Larry C. Sept. 1990. 'Three pounds of gray stuff. How the brain affects the way we absorb information' in *The Toastmaster*.

Brozo, William G. and Johns, Jerry L. Dec. 1986. 'A content and critical analysis of 40 speed reading books' in *Journal of Reading*, vol.30, 3, pp. 242–7.

Buzan, Tony. 1977. *Speed Reading*, Devon, David & Charles (Publishers) Ltd.

Buzan, Tony. 1993. *The Mind Map Book*, London, BBC Books.

Cain, Geoffrey and Cain, Renate Nummela. May 1989. 'Learning about accelerated learning' in *Training and Development Journal*, vol.43, 5, pp. 64–73.

Catron, Rena M. and Wingenbach Nancy. 1986. 'Developing the potential of the gifted reader' in *Theory & Practice*, vol.25, 2, pp. 134–40.

Cooper, Carey L., Cooper, Rachel D. and Eaker, Lynn H. 1988. *Living with Stress*, London, Penguin Books.

Davidson, J. Dec. 1994. 'Living longer but enjoying it less' in *Life Association New*, vol. 89, 12, pp. 123–5.

De Porter, Bobbi and Hernacki, Mike. 1992. *Quantum Learning. Unleash the Genius Within You*, London, Judy Piathus (Publishers) Ltd.

Diekhoff, George M. Sept. 1982. 'How to teach how to learn' in *Training HRD*, pp. 36–40.

Donaldson, Les and Scannell, Edward E. 1986. *Human Resource Development. The New Trainer's Guide*, Massachusetts, Addison–Wesley Publishing Company Inc.

Downs, Sylvia and Perry, Pat. 1982. 'Research report: How Do I Learn?' in *Journal of European Industrial Training*, vol.6, 6, pp. 27–32.

Dudley, Geoffrey A. 1981. *Rapid Reading. The High-Speed Way to Increase Your Learning Power*, Northamptonshire, Thorsons Publishers Ltd.

Edmond, C. Sept. 1993. 'Time management for accountants' in *National Public Accountant*, vol.38, pp. 26–8.

Feuer, Dale and Geber, Beverly. Dec. 1988. 'Uh-oh...... Second thoughts about adult learning theory' in *Training*, vol.25, 12, pp. 31–9.

Garratt, Sally. 1985. *Manage Your Time*, London, Fontana/Collins.

Gelb, Michael. 1988. *Present Yourself*, London, Aurum Press.

Gill, Mary Jane and Meier, David. Jan. 1989. 'Accelerated learning takes off' in *Training and Development Journal*, vol.43, 1, pp. 63–5.

Goleman, Daniel. 1991. *Psychology Updates: Articles on Psychology From the New York Times*, New York, Harper Collins Publishers.

Gordon, J. May 1989. 'Mainstreaming accelerated learning' in *Training*, vol.26, 5, pp. 81–5.

Graf, Richard G. Dec. 1973. 'Speed reading: remember the tortoise' in *Psychology Today*, vol.7, 7, pp. 112–3.

Hanson, Dr P. 1988. *The Joy of Stress*, London, Pan Books.

Hanson, Dr Peter. 1989. *Stress for Success*, London, Pan Books.

Herrmann, Ned. 1993. *The Creative Brain*, North Carolina, The Ned Herrmann Group.

Highbee, Kenneth L. 1989. *Your Memory. How it Works and How to Improve it*, London, Piatkus Publishers.

Howe, Michael J. A. and Godfrey. 1978. 'Student notetaking as an aid to learning' in *Research Paper. Department of Psychology. University of Exeter*.

Humble, John. Nov. 1987. 'Mr Mind Mapping claims you can train staff to be more creative' in *Personnel Management*, vol.19, 11, p. 63.

Israel, Lana. 1989. 'The unlimited mind – a five year study' in *North Miami Beach Senior High School, North Miami Beach, Florida*.

Knox, Alan B. 1977. *Adult Development and Learning*, San Francisco, Jossey–Bass Publishers.

Lau, Barbara. June 1984. 'Mind mapping' in *Working Woman*, vol.9, 6, pp. 110–1.

Lee, C. Sept. 1987. 'Mind mapping: brainstorming on paper' in *Training*, vol.24, 9, pp. 71–6.

Litchfield, Randall. Oct. 1991. 'How to be a Renaissance man' in *Canadian Business*, pp. 62–6.

Luria, A.R. 1975. *The Mind of a Mnemonist*, Middlesex, Penguin Books Ltd.

Mackie, Karl. 1983. *The Application of Learning Theory to Adult Teaching*, Nottingham, Department of Adult Education, University of Nottingham.

Malone, Samuel A. 1988. *Learning to Learn*, London, CIMA.

Malone, Samuel A. 1992. *Better Exam Results*, London, CIMA.

Malone, Samuel A. 1995. *A Critical Evaluation of Mind Maps in an Adult Learning Environment*, unpublished thesis, University of Sheffield.

Manya and De Leeuw, Eric. 1980. *Read Better, Read Faster. A new approach to efficient reading*, Middlesex, Penguin Books Ltd.

Margulies, Nancy. 1991. *Mapping Inner Space. Learning and Teaching Mind Mapping*, Tucson, Zephyr Press.

Mayon-White. 1990. *Study Skills for Managers*, London, Paul Chapman Publishing Ltd.

McClain, Anita. Summer 1987. 'Improving lectures – challenging both sides of the brain' in *Journal of Optometric Education*, vol.13, 1, pp. 18–20.

Miller, George, A. March 1956. 'The magical number seven, plus or minus two: some limits on our capacity for processing information' in *The Psychological Review*, vol. 2, pp. 81–97.

Mumford, Alan. 1986. *Learning to Learn for Managers*, Journal of European Industrial Training, Bradford, MCB University Press.

Nadler, Leonard and Zeace. 1990. *The Handbook of Human Resource Development*, 2nd ed., New York, John Wiley & Sons.

Norfolk, Donald. 1977. *The Stress Factor*, Middlesex, The Hamlyn Publishing Group Ltd.

O'Connor, Joseph and Seymour. 1994. *Training with NLP. Neuro-Linguistic Programming Skills for Managers, Trainers and Communicators*, London, Thorsons; HarperCollins Publishers.

Oakley, Gilbert. 1989. *The Power of Positive Thought. The Key to Attainment*, London, W. Foulsham and Co. Ltd.

Ornstein, Robert. 1991. *The Evolution of Consciousness*, New York, Simon & Schuster.

Ornstein, Robert and Ehrlich, Paul. 1991. *New World New Mind*, London, Paladin Grafton Books.

Ornstein, Robert and Thompson, Richard F. 1984. *The Amazing Brain*, Boston, Houghton Mifflin Company.

Peiffer, Vera. 1990. *Strategies of Optimism. A Practical Guide to Personal Development*, Shaftesbury, Element Books Ltd.

Pemberton, Maria. 1982. *Effective Speaking*, London, The Industrial Society Press.

Rawlinson, Geoffrey J. 1983. *Creative thinking and brainstorming*, Aldershot, Gower Publishing Ltd.

Redway, Kathryn. 1988. *Rapid Reading*, London, Pan Books Ltd.

Rose, Colin. 1988. *Accelerated Learning*, Aylesbury, Accelerated Learning Systems Ltd.

Rubinzer, Ronald. 1982. *Educating the Other Half: Implications of Left/Right Brain Research*, IRIC Clearinghouse on Handicapped and Gifted Children, The Council for Exceptional Children.

Rudin, Sherwood. 1987. 'Banishing writer's block from letters, reports and memos' in *Personnel*, vol. 64, 4, pp. 46–53.

Russell, Peter. 1979. *The Brain Book*, London, Routledge and Kegan Paul.

Searleman, Alan and Herrman, Douglas. 1994. *Memory from a Broader*

Perspective, New York, McGraw-Hill International Editions.

Selkoe, Dennis J. Sept. 1992. 'Aging brain, aging mind' in *Scientific American*, vol.267, pp. 96–103.

Springer, Sally and Deutsch, Georg. 1989. *Left Brain, Right Brain*, USA, W.H. Freeman & Co.

Stevens, Michael. 1987. *Improving Your Presentation Skills. A Complete Action Kit*, London, Kogan Page Ltd.

Svantesson, Ingemar. 1989. *Mind Mapping & Memory*, London, Kogan Press.

Traver, J. L. June 1975. 'Adult learning: you can't teach an old dog new tricks' in *Training and Development Journal*, vol.29, 6, pp. 44–7.

Turla, Peter and Hawkins, Kathleen L. 1985. *Time Management Made Easy*, London, Panther Books, Granada Publishing Ltd.

Van Auken, P. Dec. 1994. 'A new strategy for time management' in *Supervision*, vol.55, 12, pp. 3–5, 10.

Ward, Lane D. Nov. 1983. 'Warm fuzzies vs hard facts: four styles of adult learning' in *Training*, vol.20, 11, pp. 31–3.

Weinrauch, Donald J. April 1984. 'Educating the entrepreneur: understanding adult learning behaviour' in *Journal of Small Business Management*, vol.22, 2, pp. 32–7.

Williams, Linda Verlee. 1983. *Teaching for the Two-sided Mind*, New Jersey, Prentice Hall.

Woolfolk, Robert L. and Richardson, Frank C. 1978. *Stress, Sanity and Survival*, London, Futura Publications Ltd.

Wycolff, Joyce. 1991. *Mindmapping your personal guide to exploring creativity and problem solving*, New York, Berkey Books.

Zemke, Ron and Susan. July 1988. '30 Things we know for sure about adult learning' in *Training*, vol.25, 7, pp. 57–61.

Index